WHEN THE PYRAMIDS WERE BUILT

WHEN THE
PYRAMIDS WERE BUILT

EGYPTIAN ART OF THE OLD KINGDOM

DOROTHEA ARNOLD

PHOTOGRAPHS BY BRUCE WHITE

THE METROPOLITAN MUSEUM OF ART

RIZZOLI INTERNATIONAL PUBLICATIONS, INC.

This publication is issued in conjunction with the exhibition "Egyptian Art in the Age of the Pyramids," held at the Galeries Nationales du Grand Palais, Paris, from April 6 to July 12, 1999; The Metropolitan Museum of Art, New York, from September 16, 1999, to January 9, 2000; and the Royal Ontario Museum, Toronto, from February 13 to May 22, 2000.

The exhibition is made possible by
Lewis B. and Dorothy Cullman.

Additional support has been provided by
The Starr Foundation.

The exhibition was organized by The Metropolitan Museum of Art, New York, the Réunion des musées nationaux, Paris, and the Royal Ontario Museum, Toronto.

An indemnity has been granted by the Federal Council on the Arts and the Humanities.

Educational programs have been supported by the Malcolm Hewitt Wiener Foundation.

Published by The Metropolitan Museum of Art, New York, and Rizzoli International Publications, Inc., New York

John P. O'Neill, Editor in Chief, The Metropolitan Museum of Art
Margaret Donovan, Editor
Tsang Seymour Design Inc., Designer
Gwen Roginsky and Hsaio-ning Tu, Production
Robert Weisberg, Computer Specialist

All the photographs for this volume were taken by Bruce White, except for the following: figs. 1, 35, 46 (John Woolf, Museum of Fine Arts, Boston), 4 (Courtesy Museum of Fine Arts, Boston), 6, 29, 45, 56 (Artur Brack), 24 (Oi-Cheong Lee, The Metropolitan Museum of Art Photograph Studio), 33 (Courtesy Roemer- und Pelizaeus-Museum, Hildesheim), 78 (Jürgen Liepe), 86 (Anna-Marie Kellen, The Metropolitan Museum of Art Photograph Studio), 123 (M. and P. Chuzeville, Musée du Louvre, Paris).

Separations by Professional Graphics, Inc., Rockford, Illinois
Printed and bound by Arnoldo Mondadori Editore, S.p.A., Verona, Italy

Jacket: Detail of *Stela of Ra-wer* (fig. 59)
Frontispiece: Detail of *King Menkaure and a Queen* (fig. 57)

Library of Congress Cataloging-in-Publication Data

Arnold, Dorothea.
    When the pyramids were built : Egyptian art of the Old Kingdom / Dorothea Arnold
        p. cm.
    Published in conjunction with an exhibition held at the Metropolitan Museum of Art, New York, N.Y., Sept. 16, 1999–Jan. 9, 2000.
    Includes bibliographical references and index.
    ISBN 0-87099-908-7.
    1. Art, Egyptian Exhibitions. 2. Art, Ancient—Egypt Exhibitions. 3. Egypt—Civilization—To 332 B.C. Exhibitions. I. Metropolitan Museum of Art (New York, N.Y.) II. Title.
N5350.A75 1999
709'.32'0747471—dc21   99-33287
                                                           CIP

CONTENTS

INTRODUCTION

HISTORY AND SOCIETY

When the Greek historian Herodotus saw the pyramids of Giza in the fifth century B.C.E., he was told that the three pharaohs Cheops (Khufu), Chephren (Khafre), and Mykerinos (Menkaure) had built these astonishing monuments. Today, 170 years after the hieroglyphs were deciphered and after historical and archaeological research has been conducted for five generations, we do not know very much more than Herodotus did about the history of the Pyramid Age. True, we can place this particular phase of the ancient Egyptian culture, usually called the Old Kingdom, in the third millennium B.C.E. Absolute dates for the period—from about 2650 to 2150 B.C.E., give or take fifty years—have been established with fair certainty through retrograde calculations based on the more securely fixed—because in part astronomically determined dates—of later Egyptian history. A list of rulers (see page 10) has been developed from various ancient sources, such as the Fifth Dynasty annals inscribed on a stone slab now in Palermo, a newly identified, very faded inscription from Saqqara, and the king list on a famous papyrus of Ramesside date (about 1295–1070 B.C.E.) in Turin. But even in this list uncertainties remain, and a number of rulers are still only names. Following the writings of Manetho, an Egyptian historian of the third century B.C.E., the Old Kingdom sovereigns are further assigned to four royal families—the Third, Fourth, Fifth, and Sixth of Manetho's thirty-one Egyptian dynasties. The number of years allotted to the reign of each Old Kingdom ruler is less certain, because the various later sources differ widely on this matter; in addition, when contemporary inscriptions specify a particular number of years, it is often not clear whether they are referring to regnal years or to occurrences of a biannual nationwide cattle count.

Knowledge about Egypt's relations with the outside world during the Old Kingdom is based on contemporary inscriptions and archaeological finds.

LEFT:

Relief Block with Funerary Stela of Huti and Ketisen (detail).
Egyptian Museum, Cairo (CG 1392)

Pharaohs' names and images incised on rocks near hard-stone quarries in the mountains of the Egyptian Eastern Desert as well as near copper and turquoise mines on the Sinai Peninsula indicate that expeditions were sent out under a number of kings to obtain precious raw materials. Stamp seals bearing royal names and found at Old Kingdom sites in Nubia as well as shards of stone vessels with similar inscriptions discovered in the Lebanese port city of Byblos (near present-day Beirut) testify that Old Kingdom pharaohs looked outside their country, to the south, for supplies of African wood, panther skins, incense, and elephant tusks and, to the east, for cedar logs, wine, oils, and resins. Most of their activities outside of Egypt were probably confined to trading ventures of a predominantly peaceful character, albeit backed up by military force; some expeditions of this nature would actually be described in detail by Sixth Dynasty inscriptions in the tombs of officials. However, more seriously hostile raids against foreign countries must also have taken place, for they are implied by reliefs in the royal pyramid temples of the Fourth and Fifth Dynasties and by fragments depicting a siege and other battle scenes preserved from the Fourth (figs. 48–52) and Sixth Dynasties. Yet there is no evidence to indicate that Old Kingdom pharaohs annexed any foreign lands, even if some Sixth Dynasty inscriptions speak of "pacifying" outlying countries in the south in order to ensure the secure transfer of goods. All the Old Kingdom sources concerning foreign lands testify to a strong sense of identity in Egypt at that time. The home country was a secure and nurturing place outside of which it was precarious to venture. Life, in the proper sense, was possible only under the rule of the pharaoh.

Our knowledge of historical events within Egypt during the Old Kingdom is even more vague. Often the only fact known about a reign is that the king built certain monuments, such as a pyramid or a temple. About the reign of Khufu, for instance, nothing much is known. A crisis in the royal family when his reign came to an end appears to be hinted at in oft-quoted inscriptions in the tomb of Hetep-heres II, first the wife of his crown prince, Kawab, then—after Kawab died prematurely—queen to his successor, Djedefre (fig. 42). That certain disruptive events took place at the time seems also to be indicated by Djedefre's building his pyramid not beside his father's at Giza but farther north at Abu Rawash. Djedefre was, moreover, the first of many Old Kingdom pharaohs to incorporate into his name the component "Re," the appellation of the supreme sun god, an indication that an important long-term development—the ascent of solar religion—was under way in Egypt. Other evidence of that same development is discernible in Djedefre's assumption of the title "Son of Re" and in the fact that his successor, Khafre (figs. 43–47), built a temple to Horemakhet, the god of the rising sun, directly in front of an imposing rock-cut image of the god in the form of a sphinx bearing the facial features of the king (fig. 45). The eventual construction, under Kings Userkaf, Niuserre (fig. 79), and others, of elaborate sanctuaries dedicated to Re indicates that the solar religion must have reached its peak during the Fifth Dynasty.

One reason for the scarcity of historical information from the Old Kingdom lies in the difference between the ancient Egyptians' attitude toward temporal events and present-day concepts of history. Ancient annals were apt to note for each king's regnal year the celebration of religious and state festivals, the founding of sanctuaries, the creation of statues of the gods, and the dedication of revenues to the gods rather than events that we would consider "historical." The fact most important to the economic life of the country—the height of the Nile's flood—was usually also set down, and, more rarely, a notation may be preserved concerning incoming cedar logs or a raid into Nubia. Among the few Old Kingdom sources that provide information of the kind contemporary Western historians would require to write a history of the period are the lists of titles cited at length in the tombs of high officials. Many of these lists, which indeed read like career résumés (figs. 36, 121), provide invaluable information about the overall structure of the Old Kingdom's administration and society.

At the peak of the Old Kingdom state stood the pharaoh, from whom all power derived (fig. 1). The divine nature of this omnipotent king afforded an

1. *Head of King Menkaure as a Young Man.* Museum of Fine Arts, Boston, Harvard University–Museum of Fine Arts Expedition (09.203)

especially high social status to individuals who directly served his person, including the royal hairdressers and barbers as well as those in charge of the wardrobe and the "morning house" (levee) of the king. An inscription (Egyptian Museum, Cairo, JE 66682) from the tomb of Ra-wer, a Fifth Dynasty official in charge of the king's wardrobe, offers a rare glimpse into real life among the entourage of an Old Kingdom pharaoh. As recently interpreted by James Allen, the text recounts that during the performance of a religious ritual, King Neferirkare inadvertently barred the way of Ra-wer with his staff. This may have caused the official, who was acting in his capacity as a *sem* priest, to stumble and perhaps even to drop some sacred accoutrements. Immediately the pharaoh exclaimed, "Be sound!" in order to protect his attendant from divine punishment for disrupting a holy ceremony.

The king did this, states the text, "because [Ra-wer] was more precious to His Majesty than any man."

From the beginning of the Fourth Dynasty, the strictly centralized administration of Old Kingdom Egypt was headed by an official (at first a prince of the royal house) whose title is usually translated as "vizier." These officials not only controlled the country's administration in the name of the king but were also, during certain reigns, in charge of the country's workforce, which meant that all the functions entailed in building the pyramids were their responsibility. In the Fifth Dynasty, as the administration of the Egyptian state passed from the royal family to professional, predominantly nonroyal officials, viziers assumed the more definitely structured offices of supreme legal functionaries, heads of the scribal oversight of state offices, and heads of the state granaries and treasuries. To lighten the heavy burden of all these duties, several viziers were appointed contemporaneously. Many of the astonishing achievements of the Old Kingdom are due to viziers, and the names of men like Hemiunu (fig. 33), who was probably responsible for the building of Khufu's pyramid at Giza, and Ptah-shepses, vizier and Overseer of All Construction Projects under King Niuserre (see fig. 79), stand proudly beside those of their pharaohs.

Officials under the viziers' overall authority headed all the other branches of the government; in addition, they led expeditions into neighboring lands, commanded fleets of ships, and supervised building activities throughout the country. In most cases these officials also filled honorary but prominent priestly offices in pyramid temples and in various religious institutions and sanctuaries, both in Memphis, the capital, and in the provinces. Besides probable living quarters in Memphis, these men typically owned large country houses with vineyards and lakes on the agricultural estates, from which they derived the bulk of their income. Officials of this status, as well as the members of their families, are the subjects of most Old Kingdom statues, such as figures 85, 88, and 91.

For the most part, the acting priesthood consisted of scribes and officials recruited to serve in the temples for certain parts of the year. Such service was both an honor and a source of additional income. Priestesses were devoted primarily to the cults of the female deities, such as the goddess Hathor, but could in rare cases serve male gods. While their main ritual offices were those of musicians and singers (fig. 40), funerary priestesses are also known. Women in the Old Kingdom, unlike those in later periods of Egyptian history, might hold responsible offices, for instance, in the administration of the house of a high-status woman. Wives and daughters of officials, like their male relatives, often had the title "Royal Acquaintance."

Finds of statues, reliefs, and texts from provincial sites are scarce for the earlier phases of the Old Kingdom, but a small number of provincial statues from the Third and the early Fourth Dynasty (fig. 14) display high standards of craftsmanship and art. After the end of the Fifth Dynasty, as the provincial administrations became increasingly more independent and powerful, many provincial officials had elaborate tombs decorated with reliefs and wall paintings and furnished with statues (figs. 124, 126). Some scholars have argued that the increase in provincial power ultimately led to the downfall of the Old Kingdom. However, there were doubtlessly various causes for the decay of the administrative structure, not the least among them serious climatic changes in the Middle East and North Africa, which probably caused droughts and consequent food shortages in the Nile Valley. The presence of able local administrators, who provided food and security when the central administrative structure collapsed, was possibly more advantageous than destructive. Eventually, it was from this provincial base that a unified Egypt could again rise and flourish, as the so-called Middle Kingdom (about 2040–1650 B.C.E.).

Lower down on the social ladder, in what might be called the middle class, came the scribes, who would either be assigned to assist high officials or function on their own in various record-keeping duties or in supervisory positions. Certain leading craftsmen also belonged to the middle class, although many others are more aptly designated as dependent workmen of the lower classes. As in many premodern cultures, the concept of a craftsman's being an "artist" did not exist; nevertheless, the skilled creators of the sculptures,

OLD KINGDOM RULERS

	THIRD DYNASTY			FIFTH DYNASTY
ca. 2649–2630 B.C.E.*	Zanakht		ca. 2465–2458	Userkaf
2630–2611	Djoser		2458–2446	Sahure
2611–2605	Sekhemkhet		2446–2438	Neferirkare
2605–2599	Khaba		2438–2431	Shepseskare
2599–2575	Huni		2431–2420	Neferefre (or Raneferef)
			2420–2389	Niuserre
	FOURTH DYNASTY		2389–2381	Menkauhor
ca. 2575–2551	Snefru		2381–2353	Djedkare Isesi
2551–2528	Khufu (=Cheops)		2353–2323	Unis
2528–2520	Djedefre (or Radjedef)			
2520–2494	Khafre (=Chephren)			SIXTH DYNASTY
2494–2490	Nebka II		ca. 2323–2291	Teti
2490–2472	Menkaure (=Mykerinos, Latinized: Mycerinus)		2291–2289	Userkare
			2289–2255	Pepi I
2472–2467	Shepseskaf		2255–2246	Merenre I
2467–2465	Djedefptah? (=Thamphthis)		2246–2152	Pepi II
			2152–2152	Merenre II
			2152–2150	Netjerkare Siptah (=Nitocris)

*Approximate dates adopted by The Metropolitan Museum of Art

reliefs, and paintings in Old Kingdom temples and tombs were highly regarded. Such men even occasionally left their images and names on tomb walls, and many of those who commissioned tombs were eager to stress that their particular artists had been well paid. Like all craftsmen in ancient Egypt, Old Kingdom sculptors and painters functioned within firmly structured institutions, whether under royal or temple administration or in the household of a great man. Largely performing in teams and supervised by master craftsmen and scribal administrators, the craftsmen were paid according to their rank in the institution. A cemetery for middle-class officials, craftsmen, and builders, recently discovered near the pyramids of Giza, has yielded statues of a fresh and naive directness that amply compensates for a certain lack of artistic refinement (fig. 64).

People of the lowest class in Old Kingdom society were called *mrj.w* (dependents; literally, those of the irrigation canals). It was from among these predominantly agricultural laborers that the large workforces for the royal building projects, as well as the soldiers for military campaigns into foreign countries, were recruited by draft. At the building sites, the workers were divided into gangs of perhaps two hundred men, and each gang was given a particular designation that usually included the name of the king for whom they worked—"Khufu is friendly," "Khufu is powerful," or the like. Besides these dependents, prisoners of war, especially from Nubia, also performed manual labor. But up to the very end of the Old Kingdom, there is no evidence that people were owned, inherited, or disposed of as slaves.

Both middle-class people and dependents are integral participants in the activities depicted in temple and tomb reliefs. These images of life in the Nile Valley not only show the nobleman and his family but devote as much, if not more, space to farm laborers, sailors and marine troops, craftsmen, herdsmen, bird catchers, hunters, fishermen, and traders (figs. 80, 107, 119). All these individuals are rendered in their appropriate places, and although the whole certainly paraded a great man's worldly possessions, it also honored each person's contribution toward the common achievement. The hierarchically structured Old Kingdom society, as depicted in art, was not exclusive but encompassed all aspects of human existence under the gods and the pharaoh.

THE ARCHITECTURAL AND FUNCTIONAL CONTEXT OF OLD KINGDOM ART

The essence of Old Kingdom art is joy in life. Men and women are predominantly rendered as young, vigorous, and beautiful (figs. 14, 25, 26, 125). If an elderly (fig. 54), obese (fig. 33), or emaciated person (figs. 82, 96) or a dwarf (figs. 40, 41) is depicted, it is with deep respect, even awe, for the diversity of life. Animals (figs. 30, 31, 68), plants (figs. 32, 80), and elements of the inundated land (fig. 80) fully share in human existence, which is, above all, productive and pleasurable. People of all stations perform their tasks with confidence in their own abilities and in the ultimate value of their achievements. The deserts teem with wildlife, fish abound in the canals and the river, migratory birds visit the marshlands in great numbers, and the annual Nile flood comes, on the whole, with dependable regularity to water the fertile earth. No wonder that the pharaoh is depicted striding forward hand in hand with a deity (fig. 55)!

Paradoxically, this overwhelmingly positive view of life was expressed in artworks destined for the dead. With very few exceptions (fig. 14), Old Kingdom statues, reliefs, and paintings were originally created for tombs and for temples attached to royal pyramids. The paradox is resolved to some degree by the recognition that the primary function of such art was, in fact, to replicate and eternalize life, in a sense to build a duplicate world of stone that was able to last forever.

The pyramids of the Old Kingdom were never meant to stand in isolation. King Djoser's "Step Pyramid" at Saqqara (fig. 6) was surrounded by a great many buildings, clustered in groups around several open courtyards. Attached to the early pyramids of King Snefru at Meidum and Dahshur were chapels, causeways, a statue temple (at the Bent Pyramid; fig. 21), and the ritual landing stages called valley temples, all generally aligned along an east-west axis. The chapels themselves grew into temples during the remainder of the Fourth Dynasty, were enlarged during the early Fifth Dynasty, and became standardized in form with King Sahure's multifaceted monument at Abusir (figs. 72, 73). Each royal compound was in turn surrounded by numerous rectangular superstructures marking the burial places of members of the royal family, courtiers, and officials. In the Fourth Dynasty, at Meidum, Dahshur, and especially Giza, these mastabas (after the Arabic word for "bench") were arranged in neatly aligned rows with open streets between them, thus forming veritable "cities of the dead" around the pyramids. Within both the royal temples and the mastabas, statues of the kings or officials with their wives and children formed the population of the "city of the dead," stone vessels (figs. 9, 110) were deposited to ensure that supplies for the afterlife would not perish, and wall reliefs and paintings depicted the activities and pleasures of life: all in the hope that, in stone, it would last eternally.

Of the number of ways to place statues within the pyramid temple or mastaba, one of the most conspicuous was in a niche. Protected on three sides by walls, and possibly by a door in front, the statue in its niche served as the focus of rituals and the recipient of offerings. Statues of a deceased king, for instance, were placed in niches in the center of the pyramid temples, and a daily offering ritual was performed by the priests in front of the statues. In the tombs of officials, the statue in its niche marked the place where the soul of the dead could materialize and where the living could communicate with the dead.

Statues within royal temples or mastabas could also be aligned along a wall or placed between the pillars of a hall or portico. Many royal statues were placed in this way (fig. 44), and numerous mastabas contained rows of statues, partly or wholly carved out of their rock walls. Such aligned statues are usually understood by scholars to have served as participants in rituals rather than as recipients of offerings. Even less directly involved in rites were the rare statues flanking tomb or temple entrances: their main function was doubtlessly to act as guards, as the sphinxes did at the valley temple of Khafre.

The most striking way of placing Old Kingdom statues—and the most unusual in relation to practices in other periods of Egyptian history—was to position them in a serdab, a closed chamber named after the Arabic word for "cellar." The serdab provided the ultimate protection to the statue by hiding it away from view entirely, even from descendants entering the offering chambers of the tomb. The holes or slots often placed high up in the front walls of the serdab (fig. 86) were not meant for viewing the statue but rather for allowing the fragrance of burning incense, and possibly the spells spoken in rituals, to reach the statue.

In the Fifth and Sixth Dynasties serdabs often contained a great number of statues (figs. 90–93). Most of them represented the tomb owner, but there were also images of the owner's spouse and their children, either as separate figures or as parts of groups in which the main figure was the tomb owner. The statues showing the tomb owner alone are usually quite varied, representing him or her in different hairstyles, wigs, garments, and poses. The male tomb owner may stand, left leg forward, holding a staff or scepter (figs. 12, 126), sit on a high seat (figs. 53, 83), or squat on the ground (fig. 127); men are often shown as scribes, sitting cross-legged, holding a papyrus roll, and reading or writing with a brush in the right hand (fig. 102). In some cases, when the facial features of the same subject were rendered differently in a series of statues, scholars have suggested that the intent was to show the tomb owner at different stages of life (fig. 64). In other cases, the statues were clearly commissioned from different artists (figs. 124, 126).

Behind all this variety, there was more than just a wish to avoid monotony. Evidently, the Old Kingdom Egyptians believed that the personality of a human being could best be described by showing the individual under various aspects. And it is significant that these aspects are expressed first and foremost by the different ways in which a person presents himself or herself: "Look, this is me wearing my short wig; this, when I sit on my high seat; this, when I write," and so on. In fact, "self-presentation" has been identified as one of the overall aims of Egyptian art. The statue groups in the Old Kingdom serdabs unequivocally testify to a belief that the "real" self of a person is not identical with any single representation but resides somewhere hidden behind all of them together.

It was one of the ancient Egyptian's most fervent wishes, expressed frequently in texts on Middle Kingdom coffins, not to be separated in the afterlife from wife or husband and children. Clearly a person's closest family members—what we today call the nuclear family, not any wider, "tribal" connections—were an indispensable part of his or her personality. Although Old Kingdom relief representations attest to the importance of the nuclear family, the group statues in the serdabs are especially significant in this respect. There, we see husband and wife standing side by side, the wife usually embracing the husband (figs. 2, 61, 87), while the husband rarely embraces the wife (fig. 62); we see the couple seated equally, side by side (fig. 63), or the man seated, the woman standing (fig. 88), or the man seated, the woman squatting beside him and embracing his leg (fig. 91). And then the children come in, and again all sorts of variations occur in the poses and combinations (figs. 53, 91, 92). Viewing these multiform works in juxtaposition allows us to participate in their makers' insightful efforts to capture the endlessly varied subtleties of human relationships.

The strong narrative element in the three-dimensional family groups becomes even more pronounced in the action statues found in serdabs (figs. 3, 95–101). In the past these figures were usually called "servant statues" because of the nature of the actions most of them perform. Women grind grain or press half-baked bread through sieves to make beer; men stir stews in

2. *Pair Statue of Ka-pu-ptah and Ipep*. Kunsthistorisches Museum, Ägyptisch-Orientalische Sammlung, Vienna (äs 7444). See also fig. 87.

cooking pots or butcher calves (fig. 95); a potter works at the wheel (figs. 96–99), and a woman nurses two infants (figs. 100, 101)—all these activities were certainly performed in real life by servants and dependents. Yet, some action statues bear inscriptions that give the name of either a peer of the tomb owner or a member of his family. These have led to the current theory that these statues represented an entourage of family and friends engaged in tasks that would ensure the deceased's eternal sustenance and rebirth. And such offices could indeed be considered as basic acts of piety toward a dead parent or relative. Although tombs from the late Fourth Dynasty on depict the family of the owner sharing with the deceased only the elevated activities of a noble's life, the early Fourth Dynasty tomb of Itet, wife of the vizier Nefer-maat, at Meidum, shows the couple's sons (identified by name in the

inscriptions) catching birds in a clapnet, sowing grain (figs. 23, 24), building boats, and caring for the house pets. It is as if, in this one woman's afterlife, the whole world were inhabited only by her family, whose members work together to ensure eternal life for her.

The creation of action statues certainly offered a daunting challenge to sculptors: to transfer poses and groupings otherwise represented in two-dimensional reliefs into three-dimensional works. That their best efforts met this challenge magnificently can be seen in each of the figures illustrated here (figs. 3, 95–101). In a few works of the Fifth Dynasty and in more of the Sixth, the action-statue mode was applied to larger-size sculpture and even to royal images, as in the half-lifesize kneeling captives found in pyramid temples (fig. 116), the statues of figures kneeling and squatting in astonishingly free poses (fig. 127), and a statuette of the kneeling King Pepi I (fig. 115). It is interesting to note that the action of such figures usually appears to be addressed toward an invisible counterpart: the captives kneeling presumably before the king, the king before a god. Action statues of the "servant statue" type, on the other hand, were usually part of a whole group of such figures, united by their common deposition in a serdab.

FORM AND CREATIVITY IN OLD KINGDOM ART

Art historians have always been impressed by the ancient Egyptians' adherence to certain preconceived artistic forms and rules—so much so that the term "Egyptian" has been used to characterize any highly stylized, iconic art. Old Kingdom sculptors and painters did indeed observe a firm set of standards and rules, many aspects of which were inherited from the preceding Archaic Period and some even from late Predynastic times. But it was during the Old Kingdom that these artistic standards received their final shape and became the guidelines that would be followed during all subsequent periods of ancient Egyptian history. Old Kingdom artists can therefore certainly be said to have formalized, if not invented, the basics of Egyptian art.

In the Old Kingdom, as in subsequent periods of Egyptian history, two-dimensional art forms showed

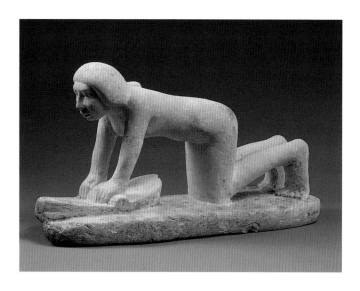

3. *Woman Grinding Grain*. Phoebe Apperson Hearst Museum of Anthropology, University of California at Berkeley (6–19766)

each part of the human figure in its most informative aspect. Thus, a figure's head, legs, feet, and arms were presented in profile, the shoulders and hands were shown from the front, and the torso appeared in a combination of frontal and profile views in order to effect a transition between the other views. All gestures and poses had to be adjusted to this basic scheme. The results are fairly artificial figurations of the human body that are nevertheless perfectly plausible to a viewer whose eye has adapted to the Egyptian mode of representation.

The proportions of human figures in two-dimensional art also followed a rather uniform canon (codified only after the end of the Old Kingdom), which basically subdivided the standing figure from foot to hairline into eighteen units, the seated figure into fourteen. Figures interacting within a particular scene were arranged on a common baseline, creating the so-called register, a basic compositional scheme in Egyptian art. In the later Old Kingdom, equal heights and proportions of figures and equal distances between them were assured through the use of preliminary horizontal and vertical guidelines (fig. 123), which were later obliterated. Larger compositions covering entire walls employed several registers stacked one above the other (figs. 106, 107), with a tall, often

wall-high figure of the pharaoh or noble tomb owner placed as a kind of bracket to one side of them.

Within scenes and registers, structural clarity was achieved by juxtaposing and repeating gestures and poses and by combining similar figures into tightly knit groups that alternated with more loosely arranged players in the scene (fig. 119). Once a certain scenic composition had found a satisfactory form, artists tended to repeat it in wall after wall, tomb after tomb, albeit with variations in details—a practice suggesting that strict schooling by copying existing images was part of every young artist's training.

The canonical character of Egyptian art is equally apparent in three-dimensional sculptures. The formal structure of such works largely derives from elements inherent to the rectangular or square blocks from which they were hewn (fig. 4). Thus, in most Egyptian sculptures the base is an integral part of the work; at a right angle to the base, a back slab (figs. 55, 83) or back pillar (fig. 38) serves to reinforce the uprightness and frontality of the piece. The history of Old Kingdom art indicates that rather than being thoughtlessly repeated remnants from previous periods, these structural devices resulted from an intentional artistic decision that aimed to add clarity and spatial definition to three-dimensional sculpture. Third Dynasty and early Fourth Dynasty works do not possess back slabs or pillars (figs. 12, 25, 33). Among the pieces illustrated here, we see an early form of a back pillar during the reign of Khufu (fig. 38), which is followed by a variety of statues with back slabs both of royal (fig. 57) and nonroyal figures (figs. 53, 61, 62). The extremely high back slabs of the triads representing King Menkaure with the goddess Hathor and a nome deity (fig. 55) may in fact suggest the back walls of niches holding statues in Old Kingdom temples and tombs. A certain architectural quality is evident in all bases, back slabs, and pillars of Egyptian sculptures.

Another structural feature frequently seen in Egyptian sculpture is the stone fill found in the spaces between the legs (figs. 12, 85, 125), between the torso and arms (figs. 88, 102, 125), and occasionally between the back slab and the figure (fig. 87). Paint preserved on some sculptures indicates that these stone bridges

4. Statuettes of King Menkaure in various stages of completion (Museum of Fine Arts, Boston, Harvard University–Museum of Fine Arts Expedition [11.730–32]). In foreground, a pounder (Museum of Fine Arts, Boston, Harvard University–Museum of Fine Arts Expedition [06.1878]) and two sculptor's chisels (Museum of Fine Arts, Boston, Harvard University–Museum of Fine Arts Expedition [13.3428, 13.3426])

were as a rule painted black and thus were designated by the artists as blank (that is, nonexistent) spaces. The main function of these bridges was certainly technical, since they ensured greater stability to a piece. However, it is significant that action statues (figs. 3, 95–101) did not usually employ such stone bridges. Clearly, the stone bridging of body parts was a feature that did not fit the narrative nature of these works.

Two other well-known characteristics of Egyptian statues in general, and of Old Kingdom ones in particular, are frontality and axiality. Egyptian statues confront the viewer head-on, with the torso and shoulders parallel to the front of the base and with the median line of the torso at right angles to its top. The spaces between the legs in a standing female and in all seated figures are usually prolongations of the torso's upright median line (figs. 57, 83, 91), and the knees, shins, and feet of seated figures reassert the frontality of the torso in a more forward plane (figs. 88, 91). In most

single statues the heads and faces fully conform to the figure's frontal pose, while each head possesses its own horizontal axis through the eyes and vertical axis through the nose, mouth, and chin (figs. 89, 93, 102). Egyptian works are, however, never totally symmetrical. In double and triple statue groups, for instance, at least one figure usually turns its head slightly to the side—a divergence from strict axiality that contributes considerably to the liveliness of Old Kingdom groups (figs. 55, 62).

As two-dimensional art had rules for representing a figure, so too did three-dimensional sculpture. Since at least the beginning of the Archaic Period, the standing male figure sets the left leg forward, and since the beginning of the Fifth Dynasty his arms hang down with the hands in fists beside the thighs (figs. 85, 125). The forward movement of one leg creates a subordinate second axis that runs at an angle to the main vertical axis of the figure and has a significant effect on the spatial depth of the sculpture: since the full impact of the forward stride of the leg is discernible only in the profile view, this clearly is the single most important feature that ensures three-dimensionality to the work. Standing females usually keep their legs side by side (fig. 25). These statues therefore have less depth than those of males, a fact for which artists sometimes compensated by representing the upper body of the woman leaning slightly forward (figs. 25, 88). In some rare cases when depicted alone, and more often when grouped with men, women often also set the left foot forward, although at a less wide distance (figs. 55, 57, 60). Women's hands generally hang down flat at the sides of the body (figs. 25, 88).

Seated male and female figures both lay their forearms and hands on the thighs and knees. The men hold one hand closed as a fist, the other lies flat on the knee (figs. 33, 83); the women usually have both hands flat on their knees (figs. 38, 53). The knees and lower legs of all seated figures are kept together, and the feet stand well aligned side by side on the base. While staffs and scepters held by men are found in stone sculptures during the early phase of Old Kingdom art (figs. 12, 41), such accoutrements are later exclusively restricted to pieces carved from wood (fig. 126). These

5. *Lady Hetep-heres*. Worcester Art Museum, Massachusetts, Museum purchase (1934.48). See also fig. 60.

wood figures also lack the back slabs and pillars of stone sculpture, and their highly skilled carvers adhered less rigidly to the rules of frontality and axiality (fig. 124).

Although the Old Kingdom artists achieved a rich variety of combinations when posing male and female figures together, they seldom abandoned the fundamental rules of frontality and axiality when doing so. Only slight deviations, moreover, differentiate the poses of figures in group compositions from those of single statues. To indicate that a woman embraces her husband, the arm closest to him is stretched behind his back, with the hand just visible at his side; the woman's other arm may on occasion be angled up so that the hand touches the man's arm (figs. 57, 87).

An especially impressive arrangement of two figures whose individual forms strictly follow the rules of frontality and axiality and whose poses are only minute variations of the conventional is found in the statuette of the Queen Mother Ankh-nes-pepi with the infant King Pepi II (fig. 114). While each royal person retains his or her own base and formal inscription, the two are united by the simple act of turning the much smaller king by ninety degrees so that he is placed at a right angle to his mother. The king's flat left hand lies over his mother's right, which grasps his knees, while her left arm embraces his shoulders. Such seemingly superficial variations of preset forms could well have produced a clumsy, disjointed effect. Instead, the artist has created a masterpiece in which two separate bodies combine at different levels, and with much free space between them, to express a touchingly dignified mother-child relationship in the rarefied atmosphere of royalty.

Since, in a work like the group of Queen Ankh-nes-pepi and her son, Old Kingdom artists could achieve such a high degree of expressiveness without abandoning the basic Egyptian form canon, it should be clear that we are generally overstating the rigidity of that canon and underestimating the possibilities for creativity that it offered. Among all the extant group compositions of husband, wife, and children, none is exactly like the other: they are all free variations on a common theme.

The creativity of Old Kingdom artists is exemplified most clearly by the sensitive treatment of details in rendering both the human and the animal body. In a 1965 article (see Bibliographical Note), Henry G. Fischer has demonstrated the great amount of accurate anatomical detail incorporated in Old Kingdom sculpture. Wristbones (fig. 90), knuckles and nail cuticles on hands (fig. 93; tip of index finger original, thumb restored), deltoid grooves on the sides of the shoulders (fig. 90), tensed muscles on the forearms (fig. 125), and details of knee joints (figs. 83, 91, 94) were rendered with great precision. Such keen observation of natural forms was transformed in their best works into a rare appreciation of the interplay of bones, muscles, sinews, and skin in a living organism. There is always a fine differentiation between male and female forms (figs. 55, 57). The lean, strong torso musculature of younger men (figs. 87, 90, 125) is as accurately characterized as the softness of the female body (figs. 5, 25, 53, 60) and the heaviness of the obese (fig. 33). Especially delicate is the treatment of facial musculature, which reached its peak in the heads of the kings Djedefre (fig. 42) and Khafre (figs. 43, 46, 47). The naturalistic rendering of the muscles around the mouth and nose in the images of these kings fully equals that achieved during the Amarna Period, which the Old Kingdom predates by a millennium.

What, after all, distinguishes the artistic accomplishments of the Old Kingdom from those of the later periods of Egyptian history? An answer to this question is most easily given by negative statements. Old Kingdom art, although characterized by an inherent monumentality, was only rarely of monumental size. Lacking the more sophisticated refinements of later periods, it was often stark and, even in luxury pieces, of an almost rustic directness; and, despite singular feats of abstraction, it was never intellectual.

Thus the "reserve head" (figs. 34, 35), which substituted the sole image of a head for the depiction of a complete human figure, is an Old Kingdom invention, but the block statue, in which a human head is combined with a largely abstracted cube-shaped body, was introduced in post–Old Kingdom times, namely during the Middle Kingdom.

Perhaps the most striking trait distinguishing Old Kingdom art and culture from those of other periods is single-mindedness. Consumed by one overwhelming goal—to defeat death and preserve life, albeit in another form than the material—Old Kingdom artists compressed the diversity of existence into a controllable number of formal concepts. Once formulated, these basic concepts were flexible enough to allow the depiction of life's diversity through variation. Thus, during this singular phase of human history, a balance was found between control and diversity, abstraction and realism. We see in the Old Kingdom a people utterly at ease with their own achievements, confronting existence with confidence and purpose. And our delight in the comprehensible directness of their art is heightened by the innumerable occasions when a tender gesture or a lovingly observed detail of human behavior brings us suddenly close to men, women, and children who lived four and a half millennia ago.

THE THIRD DYNASTY

6. The "Step Pyramid" of King Djoser at Saqqara, with the chapels of his Heb Sed (thirty-year jubilee) court in the foreground

King Djoser, the most famous pharaoh of the
Third Dynasty, built a stepped mastaba (rectangular tomb) in the desert near the present-day
village of Saqqara. Called the "Step Pyramid,"
the monument and its surrounding temples and
chapels are the earliest preserved stone buildings
in Egypt. Clustering around several open courtyards, most of the buildings were solid dummy
structures imitating in stone real buildings of
perishable materials (sun-dried bricks, wood,
reed matting).

The highly symbolic character of the Djoser
precinct is reflected in the "snake pillar," at the
right, which may originally have stood beside a
doorway. Its front shows two depictions of the
name that identifies the king as an incarnation of
the god Horus, along with alternating figures
of a lion and a jackal (the latter the animal of the
cemetery god Anubis); two snakes are carved on
each side, while the back is plain. The curved
lines at the top indicate that the pillar was probably
intended to be placed in a shrine.

7. *Doorjamb of King Djoser.* Egyptian Museum,
Cairo (JE 98951a,b)

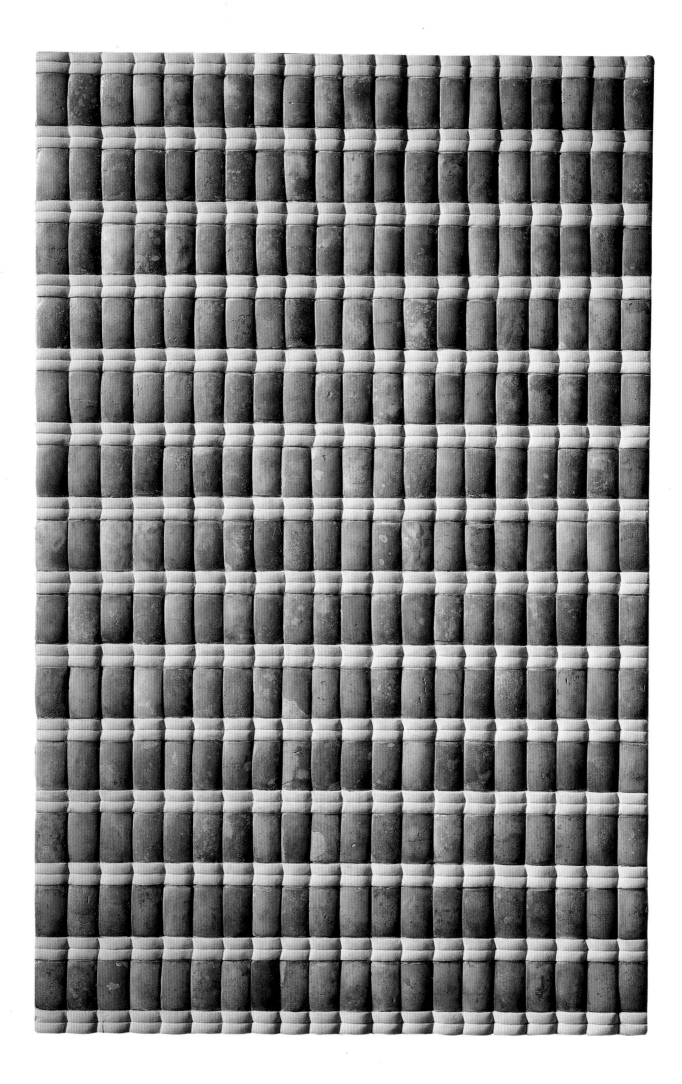

The symbolic character of the "Step Pyramid" precinct is also apparent in the wall decorations of the galleries below the "pyramid" itself and below a building to the south, the so-called Southern Tomb. These decorations employed tiles made of faience, a glazed quartz composition, mounted between sculpted limestone ledges. Meant to imitate the real reed matting that covered the walls of Djoser's Nile Valley palace, they were part of an attempt to create an eternal royal residence of durable materials for the afterlife.

The alabaster vase is another example of a magical stone substitute for a real-life object. The prototype for this jar was made of fired clay and carried in a rope net, which in the stone version serves as a highly effective decorative motif. Deposited empty with countless others in underground storerooms, such a vessel guaranteed the dead king an everlasting supply of the wine or oil that it contained in real life.

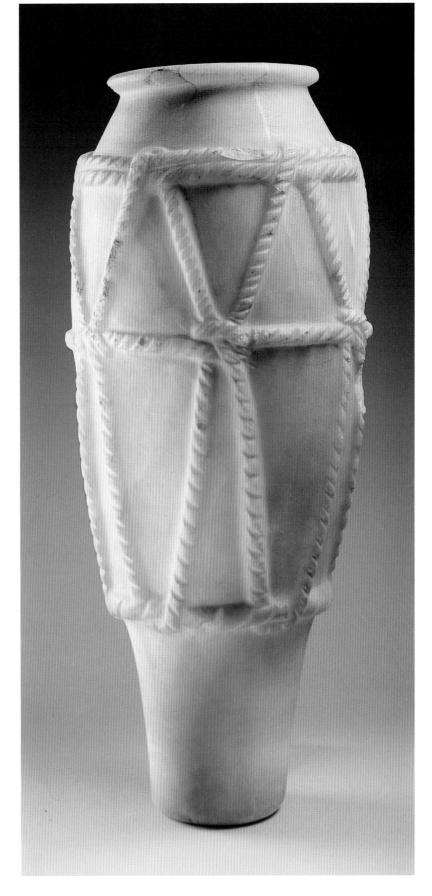

LEFT:
8. *Wall Decoration from the Funerary Apartments of King Djoser*. The Metropolitan Museum of Art, New York, Rogers Fund, by exchange, 1948 (48.160.1)

RIGHT:
9. *Vase with Rope Decoration*. Egyptian Museum, Cairo (JE 65423)

10. *Three Bracelets.* Egyptian Museum, Cairo (JE 92655–53, –56, –70). Royal or high-status persons (women more often than men) wore sets of bracelets such as these over the entire forearm.

The Egyptian pharaoh's semidivine nature is forcefully expressed in the image showing King Qahedjet (possibly another name for Huni) literally "eye to eye" with Horus, the falcon-headed god of royalty, who is identified here as the god of Heliopolis, the center of the solar cult. The king is clearly the recipient in this encounter, and the god's deep-set, disk-shaped eye is appropriately the main focus of attention. To sustain their supreme and beneficial power, Egyptian kings needed constant reconfirmation and reinvigoration by contact with the gods. Reliefs of a very similar style were set into recesses in the underground corridors below Djoser's "Step Pyramid." This piece, however, appears to have been at the right side of a niche that may have housed a statue of Qahedjet.

11. *Stela of King Qahedjet* (detail). Musée du Louvre, Paris (E 25982)

In Old Kingdom art the status of an official was often indicated by an elaborate wig, insignia of office around the neck, and a handheld staff and scepter. Hesi-re, at the right, carries the sign of his scribal status, incorporating two inkpots, over his shoulder and a staff in his hand. A thin mustache completes this courtier's refined appearance.

The official Sepa, at the left, holds a similar staff of honor as well as a *sekhem* (authority) scepter. Depicting both these accoutrements in a three-dimensional stone statue confronted the artist with formal problems, which he solved by representing the staff close to the body and the scepter in relief along the right arm. The treatment of the staff and scepter, combined with the relatively narrow shoulders and broad waist, gives the work a polelike appearance that is typical of other sculptures from this period.

LEFT:

12. *Sepa Standing*. Musée du Louvre, Paris (N 37 [=A 36])

RIGHT:

13. *Relief of Hesi-re* (detail). Egyptian Museum, Cairo (CG 1430)

15. *Statue Base with Enemy Heads*. Staatliche Sammlung Ägyptischer Kunst, Munich (Äs 6300). This section of a statue base had sides that were decorated with pairs of heads representing foreign peoples.

The statue of Ankh, at the left, is an especially fine example of the Third Dynasty polelike type, here appearing in a seated figure executed with a skill not yet attained by the sculptor of Sepa (fig. 12). By having the subject fold his hands and place his legs closely together, the thighs tightly wrapped by the kilt, the artist has transformed the pole structure into an intentionally assumed pose that expresses poise and concentration. Frontality is emphasized through the broad shoulders, and the lack of detail in the torso concentrates all the attention on the large head. Framed by the rounded sides of the wig, which directly touches the shoulders, the oval face—with its eyes highly positioned and its generous mouth—exudes confidence and a youthful trust in life. Appropriately, the amulet around Ankh's neck has the form of the *shen* (universality) hieroglyph, which encompasses two meanings, "protection" and "dominion."

This statue may be a rare example of an Old Kingdom temple sculpture depicting a nonroyal person; it was found not in the region of ancient Egypt's capital, Memphis, but at provincial Beit Khallaf, between present-day Asyut and Luxor.

14. *Ankh Seated with Clasped Hands*. Musée du Louvre, Paris (N 40 [= A 39])

THE FOURTH DYNASTY

17. *Gazelle and Ibex from the Tomb Chapel of Metjen* (detail). Staatliche Museen zu Berlin, Ägyptisches Museum und Papyrussammlung (1105.54, .55)

The main office held by the official Metjen—Overseer of Rangers and Border Troops in the Libyan Desert—made him responsible for the rich wildlife of the savanna west of the Nile Delta. No wonder, therefore, that desert animals are prominent in Metjen's tomb reliefs.

Above is a detail of the south wall of Metjen's tomb chapel, which showed ibex and gazelles arrayed in five registers; the adjacent east wall depicted an attendant of Metjen bringing a young gazelle, which is seen in the detail at the right, for inspection.

Among the earliest extant Egyptian animal representations, these reliefs display many of the features of later images of the kind: the creatures are predominantly shown in profile, the gazelles' horns appear frontally to reveal their shape, and one of the gazelles turns its head backward to indicate the presence of a hunter, an enlivening detail in an otherwise rather uniform lineup.

16. *Head of a Gazelle from the Tomb Chapel of Metjen* (detail). Staatliche Museen zu Berlin, Ägyptisches Museum und Papyrussammlung (1105.85)

18. *Offering Bearers from the Tomb Chapel of Metjen.* Staatliche Museen zu Berlin, Ägyptisches Museum und Papyrussammlung (1105.132)

19. *Scenes from a King's Thirty-Year Jubilee* (detail). The Metropolitan Museum of Art, New York, Rogers Fund and Edward S. Harkness Gift, 1922 (22.1.1)

In the detail at the left, from the decoration of Metjen's tomb chapel (see figs. 16, 17), round disk-shaped hieroglyphs identify the two offering bearers as personifications of the villages from which Metjen drew his income. Less than a generation lies between Metjen's tomb reliefs and the one above, a detail recording a scene from a king's thirty-year jubilee. Here, however, the highly complicated pose of the standard-bearer is evidence of a considerable advance in relief art.

20. *Relief Fragment with Estate Personifications* (detail). Egyptian Museum, Cairo (JE 98950)

21. The Bent Pyramid of King Snefru at Dahshur

RIGHT:
22. *Relief Fragment with Estate Personification.*
Egyptian Museum, Cairo (JE 98949)

A change during the construction of the Bent Pyramid at Dahshur, probably occasioned by the appearance of cracks in the structure, led to this pyramid's being finished with a less steep inclination than had been initially intended.

About halfway between the pyramid and its valley temple stood a temple dedicated to the cult of six statues of King Snefru. An entrance corridor leading to its central open courtyard was decorated with reliefs showing a cortege of women holding offering mats with Egypt's staple foods—bread and beer—on their outstretched arms. Ankh signs, symbolizing "life," dangled from their hands. Each of these beautifully slender women carried on her head a standard with the hieroglyph *hwt* (house), which designated her a personification of a walled settlement surrounded by fields. Like other kings, Snefru had founded such settlements to provide for his funerary cult; his name is therefore written inside each *hwt* hieroglyph.

These reliefs, the earliest from a royal temple of the Old Kingdom, were discovered by the Egyptian excavator Ahmed Fakhry in the 1950s, along with the remains of many others.

23. *Paste-Filled Relief from the Tomb of Itet at Meidum* (detail). Ny Carlsberg Glyptotek, Copenhagen
(AEIN 1133 A)

24. *Fragment of Paintings from the Tomb of Itet at Meidum* (detail). The Manchester Museum, University of Manchester (3594)

The tomb chapel of Itet, wife of the vizier and prince Nefer-maat, has yielded both paste-filled reliefs, from an earlier phase of construction, and wall paintings, from a later phase. The technique of paste-filled reliefs, first tried out here and later repeated in inscriptions on statue bases (fig. 33), involved the carving of figures and hieroglyphs into limestone in such a manner that the whole figure or sign became a recessed area, which was then filled with pastes of various colors. However experimental the medium, the style of figure composition was highly developed: at the left, Itet's two young sons, seen drawing a bird trap shut, are expertly designed both as a group and as renderings of rather complex body movements.

In the painting above, a farmer, again a son of the tomb owner, walks before a team of oxen as he throws seeds onto the earth with one hand and brandishes a whip in the other. Despite the fragmented state of the piece, it is possible to appreciate the bold figure composition and effective use of color in this rare example of an early Old Kingdom genre otherwise almost entirely lost.

This young woman's oval and fairly flat face is strikingly reminiscent of similar countenances found in works from the Third Dynasty (figs. 14, 15). In fact, the voluminous tripartite wig sitting heavily on the high shoulders and the central parting of the natural hair on the forehead date this statue securely to the very beginning of the Fourth Dynasty—making it among the most beautiful female images of its time.

The nameless woman's smooth facial features, delicate neck, small, rounded shoulders, extremely high waist, sculpted hips, and full breasts combine with the translucency of the stone to create what was certainly an image of ideal female beauty during the period.

25, 26. *Standing Woman*. Trustees of the British Museum, London (EA 24619)

27. *Two Bracelets of Queen Hetep-heres I.* Egyptian Museum, Cairo (JE 53271, 53273)

Egyptian decorative arts in general, and jewelry in particular, frequently employed plant and animal motifs. During the Old Kingdom, however, such motifs were always applied sparingly and with a measure of abstraction. While the folded rim of the gneiss bowl recalls plant forms, no direct representation of a flower or leaf has been attempted. Instead one could say that the essence of organic flexibility is here depicted in stone.

The butterflies on the heavy silver bracelets of Queen Hetep-heres I, mother of Khufu, are rendered with a fair degree of stylization, based on an analysis that beautifully clarifies the insects' anatomy. Butterflies appear along with other marsh fauna in a number of representations, and their use here may underline the role of the queen as the king's female partner in the ritual hunt in the marshes, which ensured the victory of life over destruction.

28. *Bowl with Turned-In Sections of Rim*. Phoebe Apperson Hearst Museum of Anthropology, University of California at Berkeley (6–19784)

29. With a height of 481 feet and a base length of 756 feet when first completed, the pyramid of Khufu at Giza (the Great Pyramid) was the highest and largest ever built. Its original smooth casing is today almost completely missing. In the foreground are the remains of mastabas.

30. *King Khufu's Cattle* (detail). The Metropolitan Museum of Art, New York, Rogers Fund and Edward S. Harkness Gift 1922 (22.1.3)

A procession of oxen was depicted marching along a wall in Khufu's pyramid temple, located at the foot of the Great Pyramid (fig. 29). The inscriptions above each animal suggest that these bovines, like many female offering bearers (figs. 20, 22), personify estates established by the king to provide sustenance for his funerary cult—in this case, estates caring for herds of lean longhorn cattle, which Egyptians kept on grasslands in the Delta and at the desert margins. The inscription above the ox in this detail has not yet been satisfactorily translated, but like all estate designations it included the name of the royal founder, Khufu. Executed in rather shallow relief, the Khufu oxen have gently rounded outlines that let the figures blend beautifully with the background. The details of animal anatomy are superbly observed and rendered with a sensitivity not often matched in Egyptian art.

31. *Billy Goat* (detail). The Metropolitan Museum of Art, New York, Rogers Fund and Edward S. Harkness Gift, 1922 (22.1.20)

32. *Sycamore Trees* (detail). The University of Pennsylvania Museum of Archaeology and Anthropology, Philadelphia (58-10-3)

Although inscriptions are lacking, the two reliefs illustrated here have been ascribed to Khufu's pyramid temple on stylistic grounds. The goat is another example of how magnificently Khufu's artists rendered animals. By carving the head in slightly higher relief than the body, the sculptors could emphasize the animal's knobby facial bones and give added depth to the eye. The representation of the twisted horns is a sculptural tour de force.

Plants are often treated in a more cursory fashion than animals in Egyptian art, but not in the detail above. Each leaf in the rich foliage of two sycamore trees is carved separately, and even the tiny branching leafstalks are indicated. A striking differentiation is made, especially on the tree to the right, between leaves that are nearer to the main stem of the tree and those at the very end of the branches: the latter have longer stems and seem to float with the wind.

The statue of Hemiunu, grandson of King Snefru and vizier and Overseer of All Construction Projects of King Khufu, is one of the most famous works in Egyptian art. This does not, however, prevent the viewer from experiencing a considerable shock when first encountering the statue. The man is large, ugly, and obese, and his physique must have had an even more overpowering impact when the original red paint was preserved on the body and the rock-crystal inlays of the eyes (see fig. 89) were still in place between their metal (in this case, gold) lids.

Clearly the master sculptor who conceived Hemiunu's tomb statue strove to eternalize the vizier's forceful personality. It was Hemiunu, after all, who most probably organized the construction of Khufu's Great Pyramid (fig. 29), and to erect that building in the twenty-three years of the king's reign, it has been calculated that each day thirty-four blocks of stone, each weighing on average 2.5 tons, had to be moved at a rate of one every two minutes for ten hours a day. Between twenty thousand and thirty thousand men made up the workforce, which had to be housed, fed, and supervised.

To understand this statue, one must consider not only the undoubtedly strong personality of Hemiunu but also the context in which it was created. To preserve the physical remains of a person beyond death was a foremost aim of ancient Egyptian funerary practices. During the Old Kingdom, when mummification was still rudimentary, various other methods were employed to achieve this aim; among the most important were separate wrappings for each limb, molding of the face in plaster over the skull, and covering the entire wrapped body with plaster, which was then shaped into a statuelike image of the dead person. The Hemiunu statue is perhaps the closest an Egyptian sculptor ever came to incorporating such attempts into the making of a statue, and it is remarkable that this could be achieved without violating any of the basic rules of the Egyptian artistic canon. The Hemiunu statue is structured firmly according to the rules of frontality and axiality, and the pose of the legs, arms, and hands strictly adheres to the standard. Indeed, for the modern viewer the antithesis of physical presence and abstract form may be one of the most intriguing aspects of the work.

33. *Hemiunu Seated*. Roemer- und Pelizaeus-Museum, Hildesheim (1962)

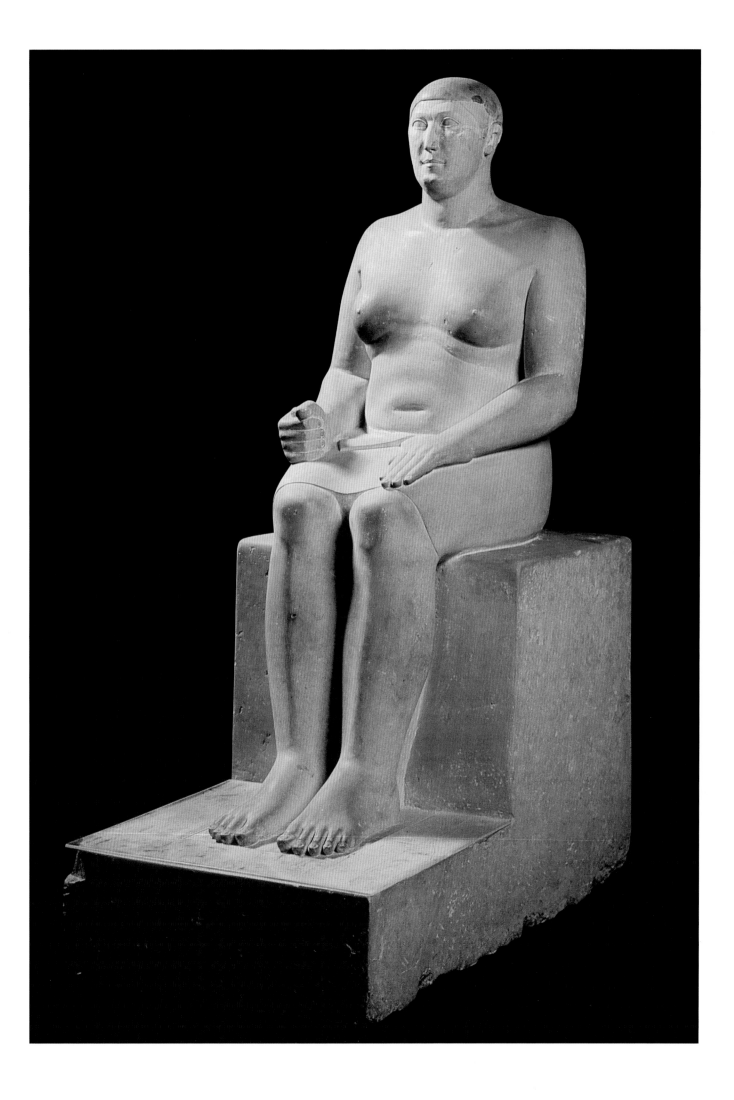

35. *Reserve Head*. Museum of Fine Arts, Boston, Harvard University–Museum of Fine Arts Expedition (14.719)

Among the most enigmatic Old Kingdom works are sculptures that consist solely of the head of a person. Nicknamed "reserve heads" because they were first thought to be replacements for the heads of mummies in case of destruction, all had been handled by plunderers when they were excavated. Their original placing and function therefore remain debatable, and the situation is further complicated by the mutilations that most have undergone. However, it seems safe to say that the heads were originally deposited near, if not actually beside, sarcophagi in tombs lacking full-scale statues. They may, in a sense, be abbreviated statues or can be interpreted as symbols of rebirth connected with the solar religion. Their austere style reduces every facial detail to its most essential form, yet each piece is also endowed with an impressive individuality.

34. *Reserve Head*. Kunsthistorisches Museum, Ägyptisch-Orientalische Sammlung, Vienna (ÄS 7787)

36. *Slab Stela of Prince Wep-em-nefret*. Phoebe Apperson Hearst Museum of Anthropology, University of California at Berkeley (6–19825)

The relief above, which comes from a group of roughly fifteen so-called slab stelae from the cemetery west of Khufu's pyramid, is magnificently preserved owing to its having been covered by another slab soon after installation. Wep-em-nefret, Commander of the King's Scribes, wears a feline-skin garment and sits at a table that holds elongated loaves of bread. Various offerings, including a list of linens topped by three falcons on standards, are enumerated in the registers in front of him.

The hieroglyphs are among the most beautiful known from ancient Egypt: opposite, we see an impressive frog (the hieroglyph that forms the name of the goddess Heket), a whip (the *mh* hieroglyph), and a feline (the determinative ideogram for the goddess Mehit). The slab stelae are thought to have been gifts from the king to tomb owners, and their style suggests the existence of a school of miniaturists who evolved a special artistic language under the influence of the sculptors at work in Khufu's pyramid temple (figs. 30–32).

37. Detail of fig. 36

39. *Slab Stela of Nefer* (detail). Phoebe Apperson Hearst Museum of Anthropology, University of California at Berkeley (6–19801)

The statue of the young woman at the left probably comes from the tomb of Khufu's sister Nefret-iabet, which also contained a slab stela now in the Louvre. The detail above is not from Nefret-iabet's stela but from a very similar piece made for a woman named Nefer. Our juxtaposition makes it possible to compare two contemporary treatments of the human figure, one in relief, the other as a sculpture in the round.

It appears that the relief has retained a number of iconographic details that were already outmoded in sculpture in the round; the tripartite wig, for instance, and the bent left arm are found frequently in Third Dynasty statues, rarely in those of the Fourth. Conversely, the natural hair on the statue's forehead, under the wig, is not parted in the center—a detail most common in the Fifth Dynasty. While the statue is thus iconographically more innovative than the relief, both share the upright, poised attitude typical of images of high-status women in Old Kingdom art.

38. *Princess Nefret-iabet*. Staatliche Sammlung Ägyptischer Kunst, Munich (äs 7155)

40. *Female Dancers and Musicians* (detail). Kunsthistorisches Museum, Ägyptisch-
Orientalische Sammlung, Vienna (ÄS 8028)

The Egyptian excavator Zahi Hawass discovered the statue of the dwarf Per-ni-ankhu in 1990 in the cemetery west of Khufu's pyramid. Nearby, in 1927, the Austrian archaeologist Hermann Junker had uncovered the mastaba and statue of the dwarf Seneb, whose title was given as "Manager of Dwarfs of Clothing." Per-ni-ankhu, according to the inscription on his seat, was "one who delights his lord every day, the dwarf of the king."

Dancing was probably among the activities with which Per-ni-ankhu pleased his sovereign. The relief opposite portrays a small woman performing at the court of a high official; she and her larger companions accompanied their rhythmic movements with sistrum rattles (see also fig. 112) and clapping sticks.

Stylistically, Per-ni-ankhu's statue shows traits reminiscent of Third Dynasty sculpture, such as the flat, oval face (compare figs. 14, 15) and the staff and *sekhem* (authority) scepter held close to the body (compare fig. 12). A date early in the Fourth Dynasty is thus indicated for this statue.

41. *The Dwarf Per-ni-ankhu Seated*. Egyptian Museum, Cairo (JE 98944)

42. *Head of King Djedefre*. Musée du Louvre, Paris (E 12626)

One of the greatest works in all Egyptian art, the head above uniquely expresses the ideal traits of an Old Kingdom pharaoh: strength of personality, steadiness of purpose, and youthful energy, all tempered by an awe-inspiring divine aloofness.

Stylistically, its rectangular shape and prominent bone structure link the work to the reserve heads (figs. 34, 35), even if none of them quite equals the degree of sensitivity with which the artist has rendered Djedefre's facial features and musculature. The corners of the pharaoh's expressive straight mouth, for instance, are embedded in small cushions of flesh, while an elongated muscle marks the upper lip at either side of the philtrum, and a soft curve emanating from the center of the chin supports the forward thrust of the lower lip. Similarly sensitive is the modeling of the lean flesh around the wide-open eyes and the organic softness of the *nemes* headcloth.

43. *Small Head of a King, Probably Khafre, Wearing the White Crown.* Collection of Nanette B. Kelekian, New York. This much smaller head, with its striking inlaid eyes and now-oxidized copper lids, is stylistically close to Djedefre's head in muscle treatment and general austerity of expression but must be attributed to Khafre because of similarities in technique and material to heads of that king.

44. *King Khafre Seated*. Egyptian Museum, Cairo (CG 15)

45. The Great Sphinx and King Khafre's pyramid at Giza

When King Khafre built the second of the three pyramids at Giza (fig. 45), numerous statues were placed in both his valley temple and his pyramid temple to participate in the rituals that were performed there. The statue at the left shows Khafre seated on a square throne decorated on either side with two heraldic plants—a flower and a papyrus—symbolizing Upper and Lower Egypt, respectively. The stems of the plants are knotted around a hieroglyph signifying "to unite," so that the whole proclaims the king as "lord of the two lands."

Khafre most probably initiated the carving from natural rock of the imposing sphinx at Giza, whose face is clearly similar to that of the statue here. Comparing both images with the earlier head of Djedefre (fig. 42) reveals significantly greater depth in the sculptural modeling of Khafre's facial features. The considerable volume in the body musculature of the seated king, whose well-developed arm and shoulder muscles are those of a heavyweight athlete, indicates that physical strength was obviously another characteristic of the ideal pharaoh.

47. *Fragmentary Face of King Khafre*. The Metropolitan Museum of Art, New York, Purchase,
Edward S. Harkness Gift, 1926 (26.7.1392)

These two fragments demonstrate the stylistic diversity evident among the extant images of Khafre. The face at the left shows a high degree of stylization. Its smoothly rounded cheeks and jaws are dominated by a broad zone of elements horizontal in form (the band of the *nemes* headcloth, the sculpted eyebrows, the angular upper eyelids, and edged "cosmetic" lines), which is harmoniously balanced by a vertical axis (uraeus cobra, nose, and ceremonial beard, now mostly missing). The slight indications of musculature around the mouth were of sec-ondary importance to the creator of this otherworldly image.

By contrast, the sculptor of the fragment above was intensely interested in the forceful rendering of such details. In the tradition of the earlier head of Djedefre (fig. 42), the muscles and sinews around the nostrils and mouth are individually shaped, only here with even more pronounced realism and sculptural boldness. The angular jaw, lean nostrils, and large, agile mouth characterize this pharaoh as a purposeful, intelligent, articulate but somewhat withdrawn personality.

46. *Head of King Khafre*. Museum of Fine Arts, Boston, Harvard University–Museum of Fine Arts
Expedition (21.351)

48–52. *Group of Archers* (details). The Metropolitan Museum of Art, New York, Rogers Fund and Edward S. Harkness Gift, 1922 (22.1.23)

Judging from its style, this intricate group of longbowmen may come from the relief decoration of Khafre's pyramid temple, where they were probably depicted taking part in the siege of a foreign city. A sense of discipline is expressed in the placement of the heads at exactly the same height, while the closely overlapping figures, identically posed with bows drawn, arms stretched out, and arrows ready to shoot, certainly convey an impressive image of military strength.

The details at the right reveal the precision with which the artists rendered the handling of the bows and arrows. They also demonstrate the boldly sculptural style of the relief, which differs considerably from the softly sensitive style of the reliefs from Khufu's pyramid temple (figs. 30–32).

54. *Head of an Older Man*. The Metropolitan Museum of Art, New York, Dodge Fund, 1947 (47.105.1)

The recent attribution of a number of nonroyal images to the Fourth Dynasty has enriched the picture of the period considerably. These images of a mother and child and of an old man show the broad range of characterizations available to sculptors of the mid-Fourth Dynasty. The woman's complacent round face and full body constitute a nonroyal female counterpart of royal images of Khafre (figs. 44, 46). The little boy, unclothed like all small children in ancient Egypt, exhibits the broad skull typical of infants. Standing well manneredly at attention, he wears his hair in an orderly braid and puts two fingers to his mouth.

The head of the man above is remarkable for its signs of age: the deep-set eyes, fleshy cheeks, and sharply incised lines running from the nostrils to the corners of the mouth. Pouches at the sides of the neck and two grooves between the bony eyebrow ridges complete this skillful sketch of a shrewd, somewhat embittered person of rectitude and pride.

53. *Lady Khentet-ka and Her Son*. Kunsthistorisches Museum, Ägyptisch-Orientalische Sammlung, Vienna (äs 7507)

56. The pyramid of Menkaure at Giza, with remains of the pyramid temple

55. *Triad of King Menkaure*. Egyptian Museum, Cairo (JE 46499)

The son of Khafre, King Menkaure (called Mykerinos by the Greeks) was the builder of the third pyramid at Giza (fig. 56). Although his reign of at least eighteen years has left no significant historical records, the sculptures that survived in his pyramid precinct are remarkable in number and quality, showing the Fourth Dynasty royal sculptors' workshops at their peak.

One group statue (fig. 55) belongs to a series showing the king flanked by the goddess Hathor and a divine personification of one of the provinces of Upper Egypt, where Hathor had important sanctuaries. Here, Hathor holds Menkaure's right hand, and the personification deity represents the seventh Upper Egyptian nome (Diospolis Parva, present-day Hiw, near Qena). The emblem of this province, the frontal image of the goddess Bat with cow's ears and horns above an elaborate knot, appears on a standard behind the personification deity's head. In the inscription in front of her feet she addresses the king, endowing him with "all the good things that are among the offerings in the South when you appear as king of Upper and Lower Egypt forever." The purpose of the group, according to this inscription, was to procure for the king the eternal support of a major part of the country.

The three figures are impressively arranged in a semicircle, with the pharaoh at the apex and both female deities—Hathor most markedly—turning outward as if to emphasize that his is the main figure in the group. The king's striding posture is subtly mirrored by the slight forward movement of Hathor's left foot, while the tutelary goddess of the province stands with feet strictly side by side. Both of her hands, the right of Hathor, and the left of the king hold the traditional amuletic rolls of cloth. The round faces of the deities are fairly impersonal, but the king's, under the enormous bulbous white crown, has remarkably individualized features: somewhat bulging eyes, loose flesh over the cheeks, deep lines beside the nose, and a full mouth with a prominent lower lip. His youthful though strongly muscled body matches the vigor of his forward stride. Faint remains of paint around the necks of all three statues and the wrists of the goddesses indicate where collars and bracelets were originally represented. The king's skin was once painted red, the goddesses' yellow.

The same facial features, with even more marked individualization, clearly appear in another masterpiece from Menkaure's valley temple (frontispiece, fig. 57). This group depicting a king embraced by a queen is not entirely finished: the area around the lower legs and feet has been only partially smoothed, and no inscription has been incised. The work was painted, however, as witnessed by remains of red at the king's ears and mouth (frontispiece) and yellow on the queen's face (fig. 58). Uniquely, no uraeus cobra adorns his simple *nemes* headcloth, which

57. *King Menkaure and a Queen*. Museum of Fine Arts, Boston, Harvard University–Museum of Fine Arts Expedition (11.1738)

has led to the suggestion that the headcloth, as well as the queen's wig, was intended to be covered with precious metal.

On the basis of the facial similarity with the king in the triad (fig. 55) and its companion pieces, there can be no doubt that this king is also Menkaure. Questions remain about the identity of the female figure, who is not characterized as a deity by any of the usual attributes; in fact, she wears her natural hair below the tripartite ceremonial wig in the way customary for human females (fig. 58). Even if her wig were covered by metal sheathing, it is improbable that a horned Hathor crown would have been added as well, because that would have made her figure considerably taller than the king's, which is not the case in comparable pieces (see fig. 55). On the other hand, her equal height with the king's assures her royal status, and she has indeed been identified as Queen Kha-merer-nebti II by the excavator George Reisner. However, it has also been suggested that since Kha-merer-nebti was not Menkaure's main spouse, the queen here may be one of the royal women interred in the small subsidiary pyramids built beside the king's at Giza.

The prominent status of the royal woman in this sculpture might be explained by identifying her as Menkaure's mother rather than his wife because, whoever she was, the queen is certainly the main figure in the group. She, and only she, takes an entirely frontal position; the king's head is turned slightly but noticeably to his right. The embrace and especially the placement of the woman's left hand could then be understood as a gesture of protection, and the obvious maturity of the woman's body—delicately indicated by such signs as the low position of her nipples—would find its proper explanation. The purpose of this statue group would then be to procure rebirth for the king.

The masterly fashion in which this group of Menkaure and a queen expresses the importance of royal females to the Egyptian king's quest for rebirth is surpassed only by the innovative portrayals of the royal faces. As we have indicated, the king's slightly bulbous eyes, fleshy cheeks, and full lower lip (see also frontispiece) are individualized features that must have had foundations in real life; this is no longer an image of the ideal pharaoh but the depiction of a living person in that role. Similarly, the queen's elongated eyes, small, sensuous mouth, long neck, and full chin do not coincide fully with the Old Kingdom ideal of female beauty (see figs. 26, 38, 89) but reflect the personal features of a particular individual. Looking at these two faces, one cannot escape the impression that here—possibly for the first time in history—real flesh-and-blood human beings have been captured inside the formality of royal imagery.

58. Detail of fig. 57

The artistic achievements of royal sculptors were bound to exercise strong influences on artworks destined for the tombs of high-status officials. Indeed since the decoration of officials' tombs depended to a large extent on the pharaoh's granting access to royal workshops, it was inevitable that the best works for nonroyal clients were created by the same artists who worked for the king. Many other nonroyal reliefs and statues must have been made by lesser members of the royal workshops or by groups of sculptors who tried to emulate the royal artists.

The magnificent female torso at the right is surely the creation of a royal workshop, and its particular similarities to the female statues of Menkaure's time place it undoubtedly in the artistic tradition of the later Fourth Dynasty. The torso may have originally come from a large tomb complex at Giza whose main owner was the Official of the Royal Wardrobe and Royal Hairdresser, Ra-wer. If this connection is true, the statue would have depicted Ra-wer's mother, Hetep-heres.

Ra-wer himself is shown in the alabaster relief at the left, which represents his head in sunk relief while the outlines of his body are incised in the manner of decorations on alabaster vessels (see figs. 81, 113). The delicate rendering of Ra-wer's facial features is clearly in the tradition of the alabaster heads of Khafre (figs. 46, 47), although it is difficult to say how long such a tradition could have continued. The precise date of the Ra-wer tomb and its associated sculptures is still to be worked out.

LEFT:
59. *Stela of Ra-wer* (detail). Egyptian Museum, Cairo (JE 6267)

RIGHT:
60. *Lady Hetep-heres*. Worcester Art Museum, Massachusetts, Museum purchase (1934.48)

These two pair statues of officials and their wives were traditionally dated to the Sixth Dynasty but have recently been shown to belong to the Fourth. Indeed, it is evident that both were directly influenced by late Fourth Dynasty royal pair statues such as that of Menkaure and a queen (fig. 57) or another, of two queens, Hetep-heres II and her daughter Mer-si-ankh III, embracing in a manner very similar to the couple seen at the right.

Although thus sharing the same influence, the two pair statues could not be more different stylistically. The sculptural depth and intricate spatial structure of the work at the left are diametrically opposed to the strict frontality of the group at the right, even though the latter is beautifully enlivened by the turn of the woman's head to her left. If really contemporary, the two groups must have been created by artists from different workshops. The works share a mood of intimate tenderness, in which the relationship between husband and wife is expressed through gestures and poses.

LEFT:
61. *Pair Statue of Iai-ib and Khuaut.* Universität Leipzig, Ägyptisches Museum (3684)

RIGHT:
62. *Pair Statue of Memi and Sabu.* The Metropolitan Museum of Art, New York, Rogers Fund, 1948 (48.111)

63. *Pair Statue of Katep and Hetep-heres*. Trustees of the British Museum, London (1181)

64. *Four Statues of Inti-Shedu*. Egyptian Museum, Cairo (from left to right: JE 98947, 98945, 98946, 98948)

The pair statue at the left is another work formerly placed in the Fifth to the Sixth Dynasty and now dated to the Fourth. Unlike the previous pairs illustrated (figs. 61, 62), this husband and wife hold their heads and bodies in a frontal position. Enlivening irregularities are nevertheless introduced by other features. Among these are the uneven position of the woman's breasts: her left breast is noticeably higher than the right, a result presumably of her lifting the left arm to embrace her husband.

The four statuettes above were discovered together at Giza in the serdab of a tomb located in a cemetery in which workmen and middle-class officials were buried. This particular tomb, situated higher up and overlooking the workmen's necropolis, obviously had a middle-class owner, identified by inscriptions as the "Overseer of the Boat of [the goddess] Neith, Inti-shedu." His statues provide an intriguing insight into the kind of sculptors' work that was affordable to middle-class people.

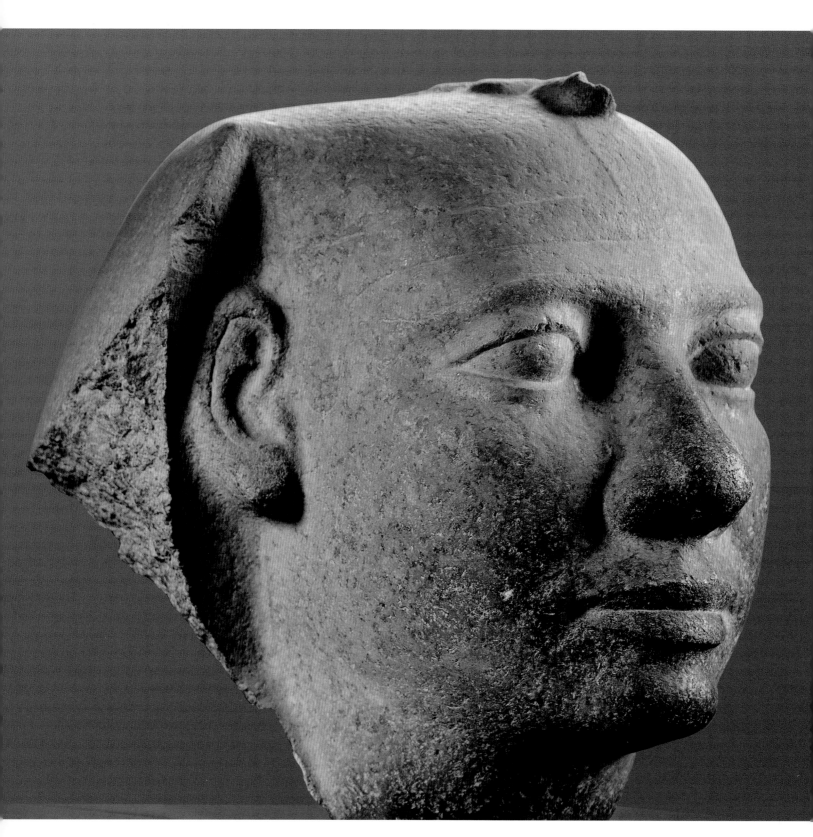

65. *Head of King Userkaf.* Egyptian Museum, Cairo (JE 52501)

THE FIFTH DYNASTY

A new era started in many respects with the first king of the Fifth Dynasty, Userkaf, who built his pyramid close to the by-then-ancient precinct of Djoser at Saqqara (fig. 6). The head at the left, from a statue that stood in the courtyard of Userkaf's pyramid temple, is the only work of monumental size extant from the Old Kingdom, except for the Great Sphinx of Giza (fig. 45). All the features of this imposing piece are conceived on a broad scale and carved deeply into the stone, as appropriate in a sculpture of its size. However, it is also notable that—despite some faint similarities to images of Menkaure in the area of the cheeks (frontispiece, figs. 55, 57)—this is an image of little individuality: the pharaoh appears here again as eternally young and above all human frailty.

The chief pride of Userkaf's pyramid precinct was its relief decoration. The illustrations at the right show representations of vigorously striding men, including an isolated officer, Ii-fret by name, who carries papyrus rolls under his arm.

66, 67. *Running Troops* (details). The Metropolitan Museum of Art, New York, Rogers Fund, 1915 (15.3.1163)

68. *Two Birds*. Egyptian Museum, Cairo (TEMP 6-9-32-1)

The relief fragment above, from Userkaf's pyramid temple, shows two golden orioles fighting with each other. Behind them are the branches of a tree as well as a rope from the net that farmers have spread to catch the birds in an attempt to prevent them from pilfering the fruits of the tree. Another relief, at the right, presents a detail of a ship with an immense sail that is being raised by one man drawing on a rope while another to the left, whose figure is missing, pushes against it with the help of a forked instrument. In the bow two men with long sticks are testing the depth of the water. One of these encourages the men at the ropes: "Sail well like this, hurry!"

All four details (figs. 66–69) are good examples of the relief style found in Userkaf's pyramid precinct: the outlines of the figures are well rounded but the figures themselves fairly flat, and there is a characteristic layering of overlapping figures, ropes, sail, birds, and tree branches.

69. *Ship under Sail* (detail). The Metropolitan Museum of Art, New York, Rogers Fund and Edward S. Harkness Gift, 1922 (22.1.13)

This statue of King Sahure with the tutelary deity of the Upper Egyptian province of Koptos (present-day Qift) is much smaller than the monumental image to which the head of Userkaf (fig. 65) once belonged. In content the piece is reminiscent of the triads of Menkaure (fig. 55). The Sahure group, however, has a distinctly archaic air, expressed in the broad faces and thick-lipped mouths of god and king and in the way the heads seem to shrink into their head-cloths and wigs. The effect is intensified by the mottled veining of the stone.

Since the sculptor was evidently sure of his proportions and rendered details such as the knees and the arm muscles with great subtlety and skill, the archaic traits must be intentional. Perhaps the image was made to replace a much older wooden one that had decayed. Or the royal workshops may still have been searching during the reign of Sahure for a new image of the pharaoh to replace the individualized representations of the late Fourth Dynasty (frontispiece, figs. 55, 57).

71. *Sahure and a Nome God*. The Metropolitan Museum of Art, New York, Rogers Fund, 1918 (18.2.4)

70. Detail of fig. 71

72. *Model of the Pyramid and Pyramid Temple of King Sahure at Abusir.* The Metropolitan Museum of
Art, New York, Dodge Fund, 1911 (11.165)

A   Roof of sanctuary
B   Subsidiary pyramid
C   Side entrance
D   Causeway (end)
E   Causeway (beginning)

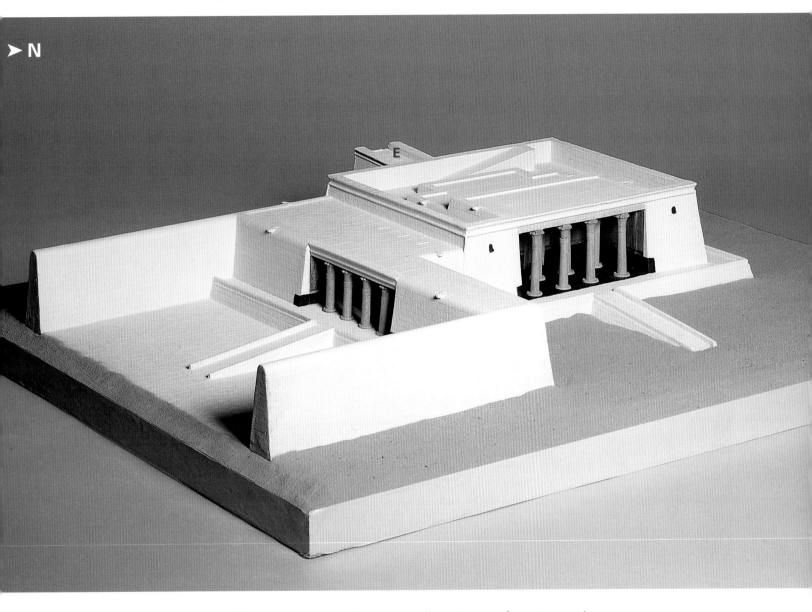

73. *Model of the Valley Temple of King Sahure at Abusir.* The Metropolitan Museum of Art, New York, Dodge Fund, 1911 (11.165)

Like all monuments of its kind, the pyramid precinct of Sahure at Abusir comprised a valley temple (above), a walled causeway (only its beginning [above, E] and end [left, D] are shown here), and a pyramid temple and pyramid (left). Another of the typical features found at Abusir was a small subsidiary pyramid, which is often said to have served the king's *ka*, or life force (left, B, upper left). The progression from the valley temple to the pyramid was also a progression from the world of the living to the eternal residence of the king.

Sahure's precinct—seen here in a model reconstruction made in 1910 under the supervision of the excavator Ludwig Borchardt—was one of the most elaborate of its type and contained approximately 300 meters of continuous relief decoration (see figs. 74–77).

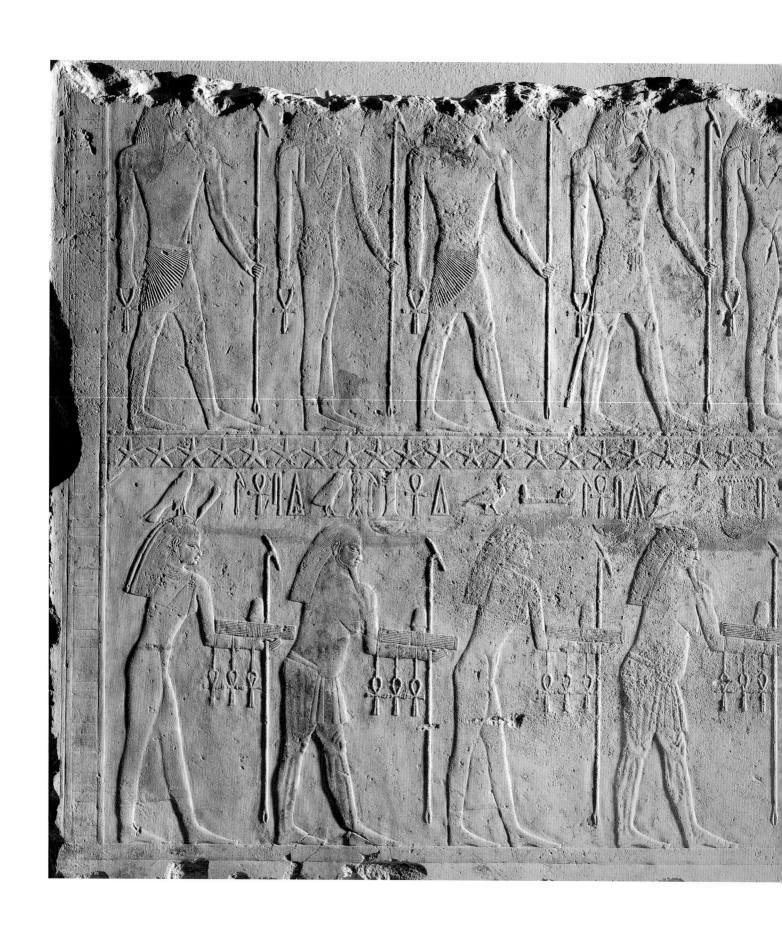

This large relief block was originally placed south of a subsidiary entrance to Sahure's pyramid temple (see fig. 72, C). Its left edge coincided with the southwestern corner of the small two-columned entrance chamber, and its right edge was part of the doorframe. The area illustrated here constituted the two lower registers of a total of four that decorated this part of the wall. The upper preserved register presents a row of deities, while the lower shows personifications of abstract terms related to the provision of food, such as "Food," "Liquids," "Offerings," and "Sustenance," followed by "West," the personification of the realm of the dead. The inscription at the right says that the deities and genies bring provisions from Upper Egypt (their counterparts from Lower Egypt were depicted north of the doorway).

All the figures in the bottom row have the appearance typical of fertility-related genies in Egyptian art: the males are obese and have pendulous breasts, and the females are slender, except for the first from the right, "Liquid," who is pregnant. Above their heads are the good wishes they bestow on the king, including "all life, stability, and dominion" and "all life and health."

74. *Relief Block with Deities and Fecundity Figures.*
Staatliche Museen zu Berlin, Ägyptisches Museum und Papyrussammlung (21784)

This impressive detail shows the second fertility genie from the left on the block illustrated on the previous pages. According to the inscription, the figure is a personification of the word "sustenance." As usual in Egyptian art when a masculine word related to fertility and abundance is rendered in human form, the figure is that of an obese man with pendulous breasts. Long hair streams over his back, and a ceremonial beard is fastened around his chin and cheeks. The fact that the beard is braided and ends in a coil identifies the man as a deity. With a beautiful expression of attentive piety in his large eye and slightly smiling mouth, he bows toward the king in his pyramid.

The exquisite artistry of Sahure's relief sculptors is amply demonstrated here: all the outlines are delicately rounded and the raised areas inside the figures are subtly modeled, the surface finish is superbly balanced, and the smooth skin is very effectively differentiated from the intricately modeled ear, hair, and beard. The eye, although not as deeply carved as in reliefs of the Fourth Dynasty (for example, figs. 48–52), is conspicuous for its size and the shadows in its corners.

75. Detail of fig. 74

Excavated in the valley temple of King Sahure, the relief fragment at the left was probably part of a representation of the king's ship of state as it arrives accompanied by running troops. The instruments carried over the men's shoulders are not yet fully understood but have been explained as military standards. Comparison with the very similar running troops from one generation earlier, carved for Userkaf's pyramid temple (figs. 66, 67), reveals the greater elasticity and elegance of the Sahure men.

The detail at the right comes from a relief that most probably flanked the main exit from the valley temple of King Niuserre into the causeway. In this image of a lion-headed goddess suckling the king, the relationship between pharaoh and deity—expressed in the Third Dynasty relief (fig. 11) as an eye-to-eye confrontation—is likened to the intimate bond between mother and child.

LEFT:
76, 77. *Running Troops* (details). Sammlung des Ägyptologischen Instituts der Universität Heidelberg (HD 900)

RIGHT:
78. *Lion-Headed Goddess Suckling King Niuserre* (detail). Staatliche Museen zu Berlin, Ägyptisches Museum und Papyrussammlung (17911)

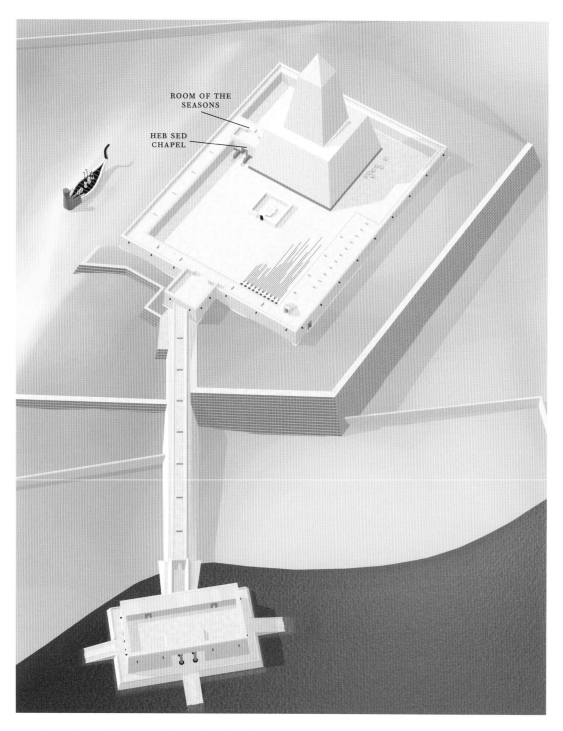

ROOM OF THE
SEASONS

HEB SED
CHAPEL

79. King Niuserre's sun temple at Abu Ghurab. Computer reconstruction by David S. Johnson

Besides pyramids, sun temples were the other great architectural form of the Old Kingdom from which remains have come down to us. These temples were erected during the Fifth Dynasty in the Western Desert, not far from the contemporary pyramids at Abusir.

The remains of Niuserre's sun temple at Abu Ghurab, shown in the computer reconstruction above, are the relatively best preserved. The ritual and architectural center of this monument,

like that of all sun temples, was a squat obelisk, an emblem associated with the sun god. The obelisk of Niuserre stood on a platform that was accessible to the priests by interior stairs. In the large courtyard east of the obelisk a monumental altar was placed, and in a small building to the south two chapels were decorated with reliefs depicting the Heb Sed (thirty-year jubilee) rites of the king as well as the seasons of the year.

80. *Early Summer in the Nile Valley, Relief Fragments.* Staatliche Museen zu Berlin, Ägyptisches Museum und Papyrussammlung (20038)

These fragments once graced the so-called Room of the Seasons, a part of Niuserre's sun temple (fig. 79) decorated with reliefs depicting events occurring in nature during two of the three seasons of ancient Egypt. This relief represents the beginning of *akhet,* the period in early summer when the Nile, swelled from the heavy annual rainfalls in Ethiopia, started to flood most of the valley's arable land. In the uppermost register the waters of the inundation (symbolized by vertical zigzag lines) cover the land (indicated by a strip of pink with black dots) while only areas of high ground remain dry. One such temporary island bears a nest of eggs, from which a newborn chick has emerged begging its parents for food. In the register below, men place ducks in a cage, as a herd grazes on the left. The ducks have been caught in a trap that was set behind a bush, and in the lowest register six men are depicted drawing on the rope that shuts the trap. The high bushes and generous use of green indicate the rich growth of vegetation during this time of year.

81. *Jar Inscribed with the Name of King Unis*. Musée du Louvre, Paris (E 32 372)

King Unis, the last king of the Fifth Dynasty, built a magnificent complex of buildings around his pyramid. His burial chamber was the first to be inscribed with the so-called Pyramid Texts, a collection of spells ensuring the king's safe journey to heaven (see fig. 117). Reliefs from the causeway of his pyramid complex illustrate scenes rarely found in other pyramid precincts. Very moving is one detail, at the right, showing bedouin of the Eastern Desert emaciated by lack of food—an image that might be meant to demonstrate the life-threatening hardships of people outside the pharaoh's realm.

The vessel above is decorated with an impressive depiction of the god of royalty, Horus, in the shape of a flying falcon. A masterpiece of the king's alabaster workshop, this flask was probably a gift by the pharaoh to one of his favorites.

82. *Starving Bedouin*. Musée du Louvre, Paris (E 17 381)

83, 84. *Kai Seated*. Musée du Louvre, Paris
(N 117 [= E 3024 = A 106])

This statue of the vizier Kai, found at Saqqara in 1850 by the great French Egyptologist Auguste Mariette, is an imposing example of what early Fifth Dynasty artists considered the appropriate image of a high-ranking official. Enlivened by eye inlays of rock crystal (for the irises), calcite and magnesite (for the scleras), the face in its quiet axiality aptly expresses the ancient Egyptian ideal of a self-controlled individual. The upright attitude of the strong, muscular body in front of the high back slab adds dignity and a sense of rectitude to the image.

85. *Snefru-nefer Standing*. Kunsthistorisches Museum, Ägyptisch-Orientalische Sammlung, Vienna (ÄS 7506)

86. *Model of the Tomb of Per-neb* (statue in serdab at left). The Metropolitan Museum of Art, New York

The statue of Snefru-nefer may seem unusual at first because nudity is not seen in the majority of Egyptian statues; the depiction of men without kilts is, however, not all that rare in the Old Kingdom (see also figs. 124, 126). Since male nudity is most usual in depictions of young boys at all periods of Egyptian history, it is often thought that in statues of grown men it underlined the subject's wish to be reborn after death. Yet one should also remember that most Old Kingdom statues of nonroyal persons were not meant to be seen but to reside in closed chambers (serdabs) in the tomb (see above).

Snefru-nefer held the titles of Overseer of Palace Singers and Overseer of Entertainment, activities always entrusted to high officials in the Old Kingdom. He may be related to two other Overseers of Palace Singers whose names were also Snefru-nefer, in a kind of musical family that recalls those of later Western musicians such as the Bachs in Germany or the Couperins in France (see also figs. 40, 41).

The following selection of Fifth Dynasty group statues (figs. 87–94) demonstrates the rich variety of this genre. Our examples show a husband and wife standing (fig. 87); the husband seated, the wife standing (fig. 88); the husband seated, his wife squatting at his feet, and their little daughter standing at the other side (fig. 91); finally we see two groups of three figures—one showing the husband seated, his wife and son standing (fig. 92), and the other in which husband and wife sit while their son stands (fig. 94). Obviously, much artistic ingenuity went into the creation of these variations of one and the same theme. Influences from the royal sphere abound, but they have been thoroughly adapted to the more intimate, mundane relationships of these nonroyal subjects.

The touchingly fresh group of Ka-pu-ptah and Ipep (fig. 87) is enlivened by the sculptor's attempt to combine what was seen in the Fourth Dynasty group of Iai-ib and Khuaut (fig. 61) with the motif of the pair statue of Memi and Sabu (fig. 62). In the depiction of Iai-ib and Khuaut, as in the Menkaure group (fig. 57), the woman's feet stood further back than the man's front foot, which was appropriate because her shoulder was also placed behind his. In the Ka-pu-ptah group the wife's shoulder is still behind her husband's but the feet are almost on the same line with his left foot; thus, in the three-quarter view, her figure appears to be leaning backward. However, this somewhat incongruous stance does not detract from the youthful charm of the group.

87. *Pair Statue of Ka-pu-ptah and Ipep.*
Kunsthistorisches Museum, Ägyptisch-Orientalische Sammlung, Vienna (ÄS 7444)

88, 89. *Pair Statue of Demedji and Henutsen.* The Metropolitan Museum of Art, New York, Rogers Fund, 1951 (51.37)

Demedji was Overseer of the Desert and the King's Hunters, and his wife, Henutsen, was priestess of Hathor and Neith. This statue was dedicated by their son Ti, whose name is written on the seat beside Demedji's left leg. The main emphasis here is on the difference between the heavy-bodied man of dignity and his girlish young wife.

Henutsen's beautiful round face below the elaborate wig and the slight forward bent of her upper body are both reminiscent of the Fourth Dynasty woman depicted in alabaster (figs. 5, 26) and doubtlessly represent an Old Kingdom ideal of female beauty. For the group as a whole, a more direct influence may be seen from such Fifth Dynasty royal groups as the Sahure and god (fig. 71). All the more remarkable, then, is the amount of free space that the Demedji sculptors introduced between the figures: it enhances considerably the atmospheric lightness of the work.

This group and the next (figs. 92, 93) represent the same family and must once have stood in the man's tomb together with at least two more works. The dignitary's name was Ni-ka-re, and he is identified as being in charge of the royal granaries; his wife's name was Khuen-nub, his daughter's Khuen-nebti, and his son's Ankh-ma-re. Ni-ka-re served under kings from Sahure to Niuserre. His statues, probably all carved under the latter king, exhibit a rich variety of positions and body details that show the Fifth Dynasty sculptors at the height of their art.

Ni-ka-re's statue with his wife and daughter is an especially good example of these works' abundant anatomical detail: one distinguishes clearly the separately shaped throat, the emphasized clavicle, the softly detailed abdomen musculature, and the flexed muscles on the lower arms (fig. 90), as well as the naturalistically rendered knees, shinbones, calves, and feet (fig. 91). Particularly delightful is the figure of the little daughter with her ponytail.

90, 91. *Ni-ka-re, His Wife, and Their Daughter.* The Metropolitan Museum of Art, New York, Rogers Fund, 1952 (52.19)

92, 93. *Ni-ka-re, His Wife, and Their Son*. Brooklyn Museum of Art, Charles Edwin Wilbour Fund (49.215)

Although also depicting the family of Ni-ka-re, this group was clearly not carved by the same sculptor who created the previous statue (figs. 90, 91). The figures here are more evenly proportioned and lack the narrow waists characteristic of the other piece. The sculptor of this group has given the faces broader lips and more evenly rounded features, but the work also exhibits a high degree of sensitivity toward human anatomy. Especially remarkable is the differentiation between the lean, tense musculature of the

father and the rounded body forms and facial features of the boy.

The play with the figures' heights is noteworthy as well; all three heads appear at practically the same height, although Ni-ka-re, being shown seated, is, of course, actually much larger than his two standing relatives. While the little boy's being as tall as his mother clearly emphasizes his importance in the family, his nudity, his braid, and the finger at his mouth characterize him unmistakably as a small child.

In this group both husband and wife are shown seated, the woman forms the center of the group, and the son—represented as a grown man—stands on her other side. The gesture of the woman's right hand, which is reminiscent of those in the Menkaure groups (fig. 57), and her rustic, broad face with the natural hair showing as horizontal lines beneath the wig point to a date rather early in the Fifth Dynasty.

Remarkable is the rich—one might almost say ostentatious—display of jewelry. Father and son are both wearing the usual broad collar, as does the mother, who is also adorned with a choker, a bracelet, and an elaborate breast piece. Together, all this jewelry contributes to a rich color effect, further enhanced by imitation granite on the seat and back slab, black on the base, and black "negative spaces" between the man's legs and at both sides of the woman's body.

94. *Seked-kaw, His Wife, and Their Son.* Egyptian Museum, Cairo (CG 101)

From the Fourth Dynasty on, the closed chambers (serdabs) of officials' tombs contained not only statues of the tomb owner and his or her family but also on occasion a number of small three-dimensional figures depicting people engaged in a variety of work-related actions. Long called "servant statues" or more recently "serving statuettes" because of the nature of their tasks, these figures are currently more appropriately identified as members of the deceased's family, retainers, and friends who are performing menial tasks as acts of piety in order to procure eternal nourishment for the tomb owner. Their three-dimensionality, which certainly increased their magical value, posed a challenge to artists, who had until then shown intricate body movements only in two-dimensional paintings and reliefs.

The butcher is a good example of the success with which the sculptors handled that challenge. Wearing a serviceable kilt and appropriately without a wig, the man grasps the leg of a slaughtered calf with his left hand while starting to separate it from the bovine's body with the knife in his right. The solid mass of the calf's body on the shield-shaped base serves to structurally stabilize the intricate upper part of the sculpture, in which the butcher's torso, legs, and arms are surrounded by much free space. As in most action statues, the man's head is not bent over his work but held upright, the gaze of the eyes directed almost straight in front. This apt reminiscence of sculpture depicting people at repose differentiates these small figures from most later toylike models of wood: although in action, they were still considered to be statues.

95. *Butcher*. The Oriental Institute of The University of Chicago (10626)

96

97

These four different views clearly show the three-dimensionality of the small statue of a potter at his wheel. The view in figure 96 seems to be the main one, since it presents the base in full profile and the figure of the squatting man and his wheel in a relieflike silhouette. However, it is only by looking at figure 99 that we understand how the large left hand grasps the wheel top to set it in motion; similarly, only figure 97 shows the index finger of the right hand forming the groove below the rim of the bowl, and only figure 98 fully reveals the occupational disease that resulted in a bent spine and protruding ribs. And still another view— the frontal—would make us truly appreciate the face of the potter with its high cheekbones, emaciated cheeks, and folds on the forehead and between the large eyes. It takes all these views together to give full credit to this fascinating image of an attentive, dedicated craftsman who seems to piously accept his humble station in life.

98

96–99. *Potter*. The Oriental Institute of
The University of Chicago (10628, 10645)

99

100, 101. *Nursing Woman*. The Metropolitan Museum of Art, New York, Purchase, Edward S. Harkness Gift, 1926 (26.7.1405)

This woman offers her left breast to one infant lying in her lap while another tries to nurse from her right breast, drawing it backward in a way that must surely be painful. A totally unsentimental treatment of the subject, the small work is a masterpiece of figure composition for which parallels are difficult to find before Greek Hellenistic and Western Renaissance art. Interestingly, its pyramidal figural scheme is also employed in the larger, more representational statue of a scribe at the right.

In ancient Egypt, writing was a means of control by the upper class, and as early as the Fourth Dynasty, statues were created that showed a prince or member of the elite seated cross-legged on the ground either presumably reading, as at the right, or writing on a papyrus scroll in his lap. This scribe has a broad chest and soft torso musculature, strong arms, and a fleshy face with a slightly melancholy expression. The well-preserved colors demonstrate what all Egyptian sculptures looked like when in pristine condition.

102. *Scribe*. Egyptian Museum, Cairo (CG 78)

103. *Carpenter, Relief from the Tomb of Tep-em-ankh* (detail). Petrie Museum of Egyptian Archaeology, University College London (UC 14309)

Old Kingdom relief art was at its richest during the Fifth and Sixth Dynasties, not only in the royal sphere but also in the tomb decoration of nonroyal individuals. In a detail from an official's tomb at Saqqara (above), a carpenter cuts away the surface of a piece of wood with an adze. Before him two wood headrests, products of his craft, are depicted and an inscription calls him "the carpenter Beb-ib." As is typical of Egyptian relief representations, the bent legs, torso, and head of the man are represented in profile, the shoulders in frontal view. Such a view of the shoulder enabled the artist to show the backward swing of the man's right arm in its full extension beside the body. The viewer has no difficulty in connecting the outstretched arm with the left outline of the torso—that is, with the man's back—and thus in understanding the pose, created before the invention of perspective, as a backward movement.

104. *Market Scene, Relief from the Tomb of Tep-em-ankh* (detail). Egyptian Museum, Cairo (CG 1556)

This detail, taken from the same tomb as the relief with the carpenter, shows a lively incident at a market on the banks of the Nile. Stretching his hand toward a large basket filled with fruit and vegetables, a naked boy runs away from a male baboon that has caught his right leg. A man whom the inscription identifies as "the Keeper of Baboons Hemu" holds the baboon on a leash in his left hand, which also grasps a stick with a hand-shaped end; with his right he leads another, female baboon with her young. Hemu cries to the boy, "Go, look, there is your property!" The boy exclaims, "Hey! Help! Strike in order to scare off this baboon!" It is not quite clear whether the young man is a frightened thief or is simply being attacked by the animal.

105. *Relief of Itush*. Brooklyn Museum of Art, Charles Edwin Wilbour Fund (37.25E)

This head of a dignitary, a high official who served under King Djedkare Isesi, has an almost three-dimensional quality due to the fair height of the relief and its detailed modeling. At the lower edge just enough is preserved of the man's shoulder to indicate that his figure was shown entirely in profile—a convention that identifies the image as a representation of a statue. Statues of tomb owners were depicted receiving offerings, being drawn on a sledge toward the burial site, or being worked on in a sculptor's workshop; this relief could have belonged to any such scene.

106. *The Hunt in the Desert from the Tomb of Pehen-wi-ka* (detail). Staatliche Museen zu Berlin, Ägyptisches Museum und Papyrussammlung (1132)

A hunt in the desert is the ostensible subject of this detail of a relief found in the tomb of Pehen-wi-ka at Saqqara. However, its three registers show only one act of violence: at the right side of the bottom register, a canine (identified as a domesticated dog by the collar around its neck) has sunk its fangs into the neck of a wild jackal. Most prominent among the rest of the animals, which seem to pursue their lives peacefully in the hilly savanna, is a porcupine that confronts a rather weary feline in the middle register. The only known representation in Egyptian art of this spiky creature, it is a magnificent characterization.

107. *The Hunt in the Desert from the Tomb of Ra-em-kai.* The Metropolitan Museum of Art, New York, Rogers Fund, 1908 (08.201.1g)

In this intriguing late Fifth Dynasty representation of a desert hunt, the musculature, horns, and skin texture of the animals are depicted with great precision. Several delightful cameo scenes include a hare and a gazelle hiding behind plants and a hedgehog disappearing into its den. The lack of fright, or even agitation, among the creatures may go back to strong influences from the peaceful pictures of animal life in Niuserre's Room of the Seasons (fig. 80). But the quiet character of many such hunting scenes also stems from an ancient Egyptian preference for depictions of tranquil, even paradisal conditions: representations in tombs were, after all, intended for eternity.

109. *Bracelet* (detail). Kunsthistorisches Museum, Ägyptisch-Orientalische Sammlung, Vienna (äs 9073)

These details of jewelry found on the bodies of entombed Egyptians give a good idea of the general character and the beauty of Old Kingdom body decoration. On the left is a necklace with elements in the form of elongated beetles. These particular insects, known since at least Archaic times from a number of pieces of decorative art, must have had important amuletic meaning. The more familiar scarab beetle, so frequently seen from the Middle Kingdom onward, was associated with rebirth, and we may assume that this beetle species had the same connotation.

The bracelet spacer above is decorated with a plant motif seen in many Middle and New Kingdom jewelry pieces—the acacia pod. The acacia was a sacred tree of the goddess Sakhmet, and the Pyramid Texts (fig. 117) speak of kings' having been born under the tree; again a connection with birth and rebirth seems indicated. To what extent the kind of jewelry here illustrated was also worn by living people is unknown. The insect necklace was owned by a woman, the bracelet by a man: the wearing of jewelry was obviously not always a matter of gender in the Old Kingdom.

108. *Necklace* (detail). Universität Leipzig, Ägyptisches Museum (3770)

111. *Basin with Handle.* Universität Leipzig, Ägyptisches Museum (2169)

The vessel at the left is another masterpiece from the royal alabaster workshops (see fig. 81). The artist has fully exploited the beautiful veining of the stone material so that the neck and shoulder are formed from semitranslucent, creamy white stone while the body seems to be covered by a variety of undulating veins of orange, light brown, and a darker brown color. Although part of the stone material, the few patches of nontranslucent chalk-white material look as if they were applied by a painter's brush.

Like the alabaster jar, the copper vessel (dated to the Sixth Dynasty) was found in a tomb. When excavated, near the head end of a sarcophagus, it was still partly filled with a gray-brown mass, and a copper spatula rested inside. The material it contained was probably a cosmetic ointment, which was applied with the help of the instrument. Twisted handles such as the one here are extremely rare: the only known parallel was found in the tomb of the Second Dynasty king Khasekhemui.

110. *Jar.* The Metropolitan Museum of Art, New York, Rogers Fund, 1921 (21.2.8)

THE SIXTH DYNASTY

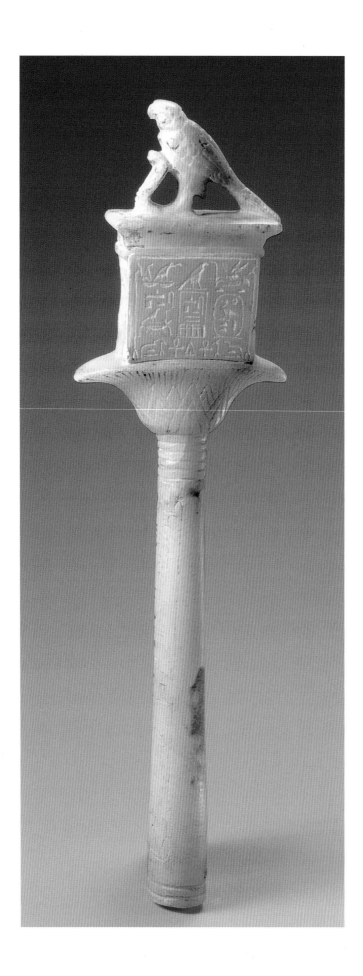

This delicate example of the rattle-type musical instrument called a sistrum is termed a naos sistrum because it has a sound box in the shape of a shrine (naos) with a cornice and torus molding. Copper wires were once inserted into two holes that perforate the naos horizontally, and small copper disks were strung loosely onto the wires. When shaken, the instrument produced a buzzing sound.

This naos sistrum, one of the earliest extant, is special not only for being made of alabaster (sistrums were usually made of metal) but also for bearing the name of a pharaoh—Teti, first king of the Sixth Dynasty—which is incised on the sound box. A small three-dimensional falcon-shaped figure of Horus, god of kingship, standing behind a royal cobra tops the instrument; on the stem, which has the form of a papyrus stalk with its umbel, Teti's name is again incised, together with the epithet "beloved by [the goddess] Hathor, mistress of Dendara." An image of the goddess smelling a lotus flower, seen here on the right, is part of this inscription. The sistrum was presumably a gift by the king to Hathor.

112, 113. *Sistrum Inscribed with the Name of King Teti*. The Metropolitan Museum of Art, New York, Purchase, Edward S. Harkness Gift, 1926 (26.7.1450)

The sculpture on the right depicts King Pepi I kneeling and presenting globular pots with wine or water to a deity; that on the left shows his wife Queen Ankh-nes-meryre II holding their son Pepi II on her lap. Both works are strikingly intricate three-dimensional compositions.

The kneeling king's arms are fully detached from his torso, and there is also open space between his knees and feet. In the queen's group very little stone bridging connects the torsos and limbs of the figures, and the infant king's upper body is almost entirely separated from his mother's. This amount of separation, highly unusual for Egyptian stone statuary, has been achieved by skillful drilling. It confers on the sculptures a fragility more reminiscent of luxury objects and accords well with the somewhat mannered style, which is especially noticeable in the kneeling king's narrow waist and masklike face and in the elongated limbs of the alabaster figures. The artists who created these representations of royalty saw the pharaoh and queen as creatures of an eerie otherworldliness.

LEFT:
114. *Queen Ankh-nes-meryre II and Her Son King Pepi II*. Brooklyn Museum of Art, Charles Edwin Wilbour Fund (39.119)

RIGHT:
115. *King Pepi I Kneeling*. Brooklyn Museum of Art, Charles Edwin Wilbour Fund (39.121)

Statues of bound prisoners such as the one here have been found in several pyramid precincts. Usually their heads are severed; this figure's neck and part of the shoulders were also destroyed and have been restored. It is thought that the statues were once lined up in a hall of the pyramid temple in order to be ritually executed during certain cultic performances.

Like most of its type, this statue is rather cursorily executed, but the sculptor has carved one particular item in great detail: the rope that binds the man's arms just above the elbows. The binding is, in fact, disproportionately strong, and the whole composition of the figure—the forward bend of the torso and head as well as the painful contraction of the shoulders—is developed from this central motif. Subdued strength and dignified submission before an inescapable fate are expressed in every line of the sculpture.

116. *Kneeling Captive*. The Metropolitan Museum of Art, New York, Fletcher Fund, 1947 (47.2)

117. *Fragment with Pyramid Texts* (detail). Petrie Museum of Egyptian Archaeology, University College London (UC 14540)

Beginning with the Fifth Dynasty ruler Unis, certain spells called Pyramid Texts were carved in well-regulated columns onto the walls of the subterranean chambers of royal pyramids. Drawn partly from collections of older text material (and sometimes from very ancient sources), some of the spells provide glimpses of early, primitive funerary beliefs, as when the king is said to devour the gods in order to gain their power. Others, of a more contemporary religious character, concern the king's ascent to the northern star or his joining the sun god, while still others mention Osiris and his resurrection. The text on the fragment above was written for a king Pepi—either Pepi I or II—and contains sentences such as: "The house of this Pepi belonging to the sky [will not perish; the seat of this Pepi belonging to the earth] cannot be destroyed."

The cosmetic vases in the form of female monkeys with babies, on the right, are inscribed with the names of Kings Merenre (left) and Pepi I (right). Vases such as these were gifts from the pharaoh to favorites on the occasion of his thirty-year jubilee (Heb Sed).

118. *Two Vases in the Shape of Mother Monkeys and Their Young.* Left: The Metropolitan Museum of
Art, New York, Theodore M. Davis Collection, Bequest of Theodore M. Davis, 1915 (30.8.134).
Right: The Metropolitan Museum of Art, New York, Purchase, Joseph Pulitzer Bequest, Fletcher
Fund, and Lila Acheson Wallace, Russell and Judy Carson, William Kelly Simpson, and Vaughn
Foundation Gifts, in honor of Henry George Fischer, 1992 (1992.338)

119. *Fishermen and Herdsmen with Their Animals.* The Detroit Institute of Arts, City of Detroit Purchase (30.371)

The relief on these two blocks furnishes a prime example of the kinds of scenes depicted in many tombs of officials during the Fifth and Sixth Dynasties. On the left a herd of cattle is crossing a canal or river branch; on the right several fishermen have cast their net and are making a good catch. The two scenes are effectively linked by the common expanse of water that appears as a blue zone at the bottom of the relief. The placement of the legs of the cattle and the herds-men in front of this blue zone indicates that they are wading through the water, while the fishermen's standing on a narrow solid strip above the blue signifies that they are on the bank of the waterway. It is typical of the largely conceptual character of Egyptian art that landscape and location are thus represented by a few emblematic props rather than by a visually conceived image.

The effectiveness of the present composition relies on the juxtaposition of the rather dense

group of bovines and the complex interplay of the fishermen's legs. In such a context, the two upright single figures stand out all the more: the herdsman with a stick on the left, who coaxes the herd into the water, and the man in the center, who carries a calf on his back to induce the mother cow to follow. Sensitive details—such as the cow and calf touching their tongues together and another bovine taking a sip of water—enrich the bucolic scene and lend it emotion.

The sense of real life is further enhanced by the abundance of other precisely observed details. Heavy stone sinkers are, for instance, depicted at the bottom of the fishermen's net, while light wood swimmers are affixed to its top. The fish species, all of which are common to the Nile, are well differentiated; from left to right, they are a mullet, an elephant-snout fish, a bolti, and another type of elephant-snout fish.

121. *False-Door Stela from the Tomb of Metjetji.* The Metropolitan Museum of Art, New York, Gift of Mr. and Mrs. J. J. Klejman, 1964 (64.100)

The fragment on the left comes from a tomb relief representing offerings piled up in front of the deceased. This seemingly random depiction of slaughtered ducks, vegetables, and fruits tumbling one over the other may remind the modern viewer of still lifes depicting the spoils of the hunt.

Shown above is the upper part of a so-called false door, a stylized depiction of an actual doorway that marked the place in the tomb where relatives of the deceased could leave

offerings, and the deceased could emerge to receive them. The inscribed lintel of the symbolic door appears in the center; the deeper shadow at the lower end of the illustration indicates the uppermost part of the symbolic nichelike door opening, which is topped by a horizontal rectangle meant to duplicate the rolled-up awning that closed real-life doorways. The tomb owner, a man called Metjetji, is shown twice—seated, on the slab in the windowlike recess, and standing, on the right.

120. *Still Life: Offerings for the Deceased.* The Detroit Institute of Arts, Founders Society Purchase, Hill Memorial Fund (76.5)

123. *Wall Painting from the Tomb of Metjetji.* Musée du Louvre, Paris (E 25512)

At the left, the upper part of another figure of Metjetji (see fig. 121) demonstrates well a type and style of relief that became common during the later Old Kingdom. It is executed in so-called sunk relief, in which the background is not carved away around the figure. First appearing in the Fourth Dynasty, this type of relief was used most frequently during the Sixth. The image of Metjetji is preternaturally elongated (as in figs. 121 and 122), musculature is sparsely indicated, and the main emphasis is on differences in surface texture on body, jewelry, and hair.

The same attention to figural outlines is also discernible in the example from Metjetji's wall paintings above. Although inventive, the poses and groupings appear frozen to heraldic configurations—an impression that is not alleviated by the fine brushwork on the animals' skin. It seems fitting that the painters made ample use of vertical guidelines in composing their scene.

122. *Fragment from the Facade of the Tomb of Metjetji* (detail). Royal Ontario Museum, Toronto (953.116.1)

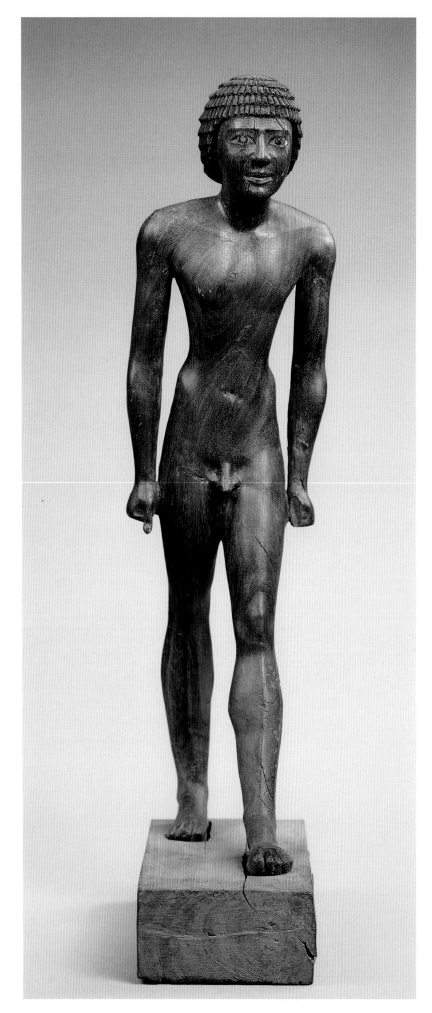

The statuette at the left is a superb example of Sixth Dynasty wood carving. Executed in hard African wood, the young man shows the slender proportions and slim waist of the Sixth Dynasty ideal. The lean musculature is very sensitively rendered, and the artist's exceptionally fine sense of bone structure can be seen in the way he developed the forward-striding pose from the delicately emphasized hips and knees. The result is a strikingly realistic impression of movement, encompassing even the head, which is turned in the direction of the advancing leg.

The brightly painted limestone statue at the right compares not unfavorably with the wood masterpiece, even though it displays the conventional "shadow" bridges between the torso and arms and between the two legs. This young man has the same narrow waist and somewhat spindly arms and legs as the other youth, but greater emphasis on the frontality of his broad-shouldered torso has resulted in a more dignified expression. Each man wears a close-fitting wig, which in the case of the limestone work leaves the ears visible. The faces are remarkably different, with the youth at the right having more fleshy features and a more somber bearing. There is a remarkable nervous swiftness to both figures.

LEFT:
124. *Meryre-ha-ishetef Standing*. Trustees of the British Museum, London (EA 55722)

RIGHT:
125. *Atjema Standing*. Egyptian Museum, Cairo (CG 99)

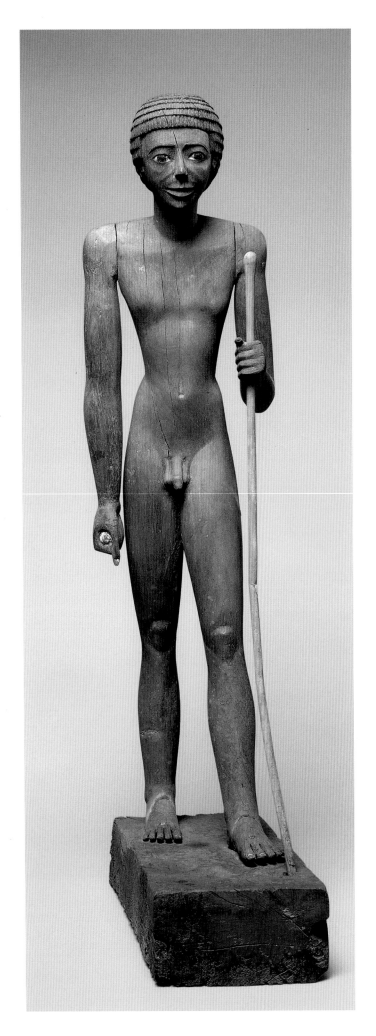

The sculptural style represented by these two works from the late Old Kingdom used to be described as a degeneration of Old Kingdom art but has recently received more appreciation as it has come to be seen as a style in its own right. Scholars now argue that such emaciated bodies, stylized musculature, and masklike facial features are the result of several factors: a reorientation toward a less physical understanding of human existence, a tendency toward freer artistic expression, and an attempt to revive the artistic language of the early Old Kingdom.

The wood statue at the left—found, interestingly enough, in the same tomb as the lively wood statuette (fig. 124)—certainly qualifies as an almost antinaturalistic work. The thin body ideal is here transformed into an abstraction of the human body, and the rigid facial features have a ghostly appearance. The statue at the right retains a traditional complex pose from the Fifth Dynasty (see figs. 100, 101), but the cutting of the hard stone is harsh and the face has an archaic axiality. Even if no longer considered as diminished in quality, figures such as these clearly mark the end of Old Kingdom art.

LEFT:
126. *Meryre-ha-ishetef with a Staff*. Ny Carlsberg Glyptotek, Copenhagen (AEIN 1560)

RIGHT:
127. *Prince Tjau Seated on the Ground*. Egyptian Museum, Cairo (CG 120)

LIST OF PLATES

For specific dates of pharaohs' reigns, see chart on page 10.

p. 6. *Relief Block with Funerary Stela of Huti and Ketisen.* Saqqara; Fourth Dynasty, no later than reign of Djedefre. Limestone, h. 48 cm (19 in.). Egyptian Museum, Cairo (CG 1392)

1. *Head of King Menkaure as a Young Man.* Giza; Fourth Dynasty, reign of Menkaure. Egyptian alabaster, h. 28.5 cm (11¼ in.). Museum of Fine Arts, Boston, Harvard University–Museum of Fine Arts Expedition (09.203)

2. *Pair Statue of Ka-pu-ptah and Ipep.* Giza; Fifth Dynasty. Painted limestone, h. 56 cm (22 in.). Kunsthistorisches Museum, Ägyptisch-Orientalische Sammlung, Vienna (ÄS 7444)

3. *Woman Grinding Grain.* Giza; Fifth Dynasty? Limestone with remains of paint, h. 18 cm (7⅛ in.). Phoebe Apperson Hearst Museum of Anthropology, University of California at Berkeley (6–19766)

4. *Statuettes of King Menkaure in various stages of completion, with sculptor's chisels and pounder.* Statuettes: Giza; Fourth Dynasty, reign of Menkaure. Diorite, h. ca. 35.2 cm (13⅞ in.). Museum of Fine Arts, Boston, Harvard University–Museum of Fine Arts Expedition (11.730, 11.731, 11.732). Stone pounder: Giza; Fourth to Fifth Dynasty. Granite, l. 19.5 cm (7⅝ in.). Museum of Fine Arts, Boston, Harvard University–Museum of Fine Arts Expedition (06.1878). Chisels: Giza; Sixth Dynasty. Copper, l. 12.2, 13 cm (4¾, 5⅛ in.). Museum of Fine Arts, Boston, Harvard University–Museum of Fine Arts Expedition (13.3428, 13.3426).

5. *Female Torso, probably Lady Hetep-heres.* Giza; Fourth Dynasty, reign of Shepseskaf, or Fifth Dynasty, reign of Neferirkare. Limestone, h. 137 cm (54 in.). Worcester Art Museum, Massachusetts, Museum purchase (1934.48)

6. The "Step Pyramid" of King Djoser, Saqqara

7. *Pillar or Doorjamb of King Djoser.* Saqqara; Third Dynasty. Limestone, total h. 211.3 cm (83¼ in.). Egyptian Museum, Cairo (JE 98951a,b)

8. *Wall Decoration from the Funerary Apartments of King Djoser.* Saqqara; Third Dynasty, reign of Djoser. Blue-green Egyptian faience, h. 113 cm (44½ in.); each tile, ca. 6.5 × 4 cm (2½ × 1⅝ in.). The Metropolitan Museum of Art, New York, Rogers Fund, by exchange, 1948 (48.160.1)

9. *Vase with Rope Decoration.* From the underground galleries, Djoser precinct, Saqqara; Third Dynasty. Egyptian alabaster, h. 63.5 cm (25 in.). Egyptian Museum, Cairo (JE 65423)

10. *Three Bracelets.* Saqqara; Third Dynasty, reign of Sekhemkhet. Gold, diam. 5.6–7.5 cm (2¼–3 in.). Egyptian Museum, Cairo (JE 92655–53, –56, –70)

11. *Stela of King Qahedjet.* Third Dynasty. Fine-grained limestone, h. 50.5 cm (19⅞ in.). Musée du Louvre, Paris (E 25982)

12. *Sepa Standing.* Probably North Saqqara; Third Dynasty, before or during reign of Djoser. Painted limestone, h. 165 cm (65 in.). Musée du Louvre, Paris (N 37 [=A 36])

13. *Relief of Hesi-re.* Saqqara; Third Dynasty, reign of Djoser. Acacia wood, h. 86 cm (33⅞ in.). Egyptian Museum, Cairo (CG 1430)

14. *Ankh Seated with Clasped Hands.* Beit Khallaf; Third Dynasty, reign of Djoser. Gray porphyroid granite, h. 62.5 cm (24⅝ in.). Musée du Louvre, Paris (N 40 [=A 39])

15. *Statue Base with Enemy Heads.* Third Dynasty. Egyptian alabaster, h. 19.5 cm (7¾ in.). Staatliche Sammlung Ägyptischer Kunst, Munich (ÄS 6300)

16–18. *Relief Blocks from the Tomb Chapel of Metjen.* Saqqara; Fourth Dynasty, reign of Snefru. Limestone, h., ca. 50.5 cm (19⅞ in.). Staatliche Museen zu Berlin, Ägyptisches Museum und Papyrussammlung ([16] 1105.85, [17] 1105.54, .55, [18] 1105.132)

19. *Scenes from a King's Thirty-Year Jubilee.* Reused at Lisht North; Fourth Dynasty, probably reign of Snefru. Limestone, h. 73.6 cm (29 in.). The Metropolitan Museum of Art, New York, Rogers Fund and Edward S. Harkness Gift, 1922 (22.1.1)

20. *Relief Fragment with Estate Personifications.* Dahshur; Fourth Dynasty, reign of Snefru. Limestone with faint remains of paint, h. 55 cm (21⅝ in.). Egyptian Museum, Cairo (JE 98950)

21. The Bent Pyramid of King Snefru, Dahshur

22. *Relief Fragment with Estate Personification.* Dahshur; Fourth Dynasty, reign of Snefru. Limestone with faint remains of paint, h. 93 cm (36⅝ in.). Egyptian Museum, Cairo (JE 98949)

23. *Paste-Filled Relief from the Tomb of Itet at Meidum.* Fourth Dynasty, reign of Snefru. Limestone with paste fill, h. 100 cm (39⅜ in.). Ny Carlsberg Glyptotek, Copenhagen (AEIN 1133 A)

24. *Fragment of Paintings from the Tomb of Itet at Meidum.* Fourth Dynasty, reign of Snefru. Tempera on thin layer of fine plaster over coarser plaster mixed with chaff, h. 41 cm (16⅛ in.). The Manchester Museum, University of Manchester (3594)

25, 26. *Standing Woman.* Early Fourth Dynasty. Egyptian alabaster with faint remains of paint, h. 48.7 cm (19¼ in.). Trustees of the British Museum, London (EA 24619)

27. *Two Bracelets of Queen Hetep-heres I.* Giza; Fourth Dynasty, reign of Senfru to early reign of Khufu. Silver, turquoise, lapis lazuli, and carnelian, diam. 8.8–9 cm (3½–3⅝ in.). Egyptian Museum, Cairo (JE 53271, JE 53273)

28. *Bowl with Turned-In Sections of Rim.* Giza; Fourth Dynasty or earlier. Gneiss, diam. 20 cm (7⅞ in.). Phoebe Apperson Hearst Museum of Anthropology, University of California at Berkeley (6–19784)

29. The Great Pyramid of Khufu, Giza

30. *King Khufu's Cattle.* Reused at Lisht North; Fourth Dynasty, reign of Khufu. Limestone, h. 46 cm (18⅛ in.). The Metropolitan Museum of Art, New York, Rogers Fund and Edward S. Harkness Gift, 1922 (22.1.3)

31. *Billy Goat.* Reused at Lisht North; Fourth Dynasty, probably reign of Khufu. Limestone, h. 28 cm (11 in.). The Metropolitan Museum of Art, New York, Rogers Fund and Edward S. Harkness Gift, 1922 (22.1.20)

32. *Sycamore Trees.* Reused at Lisht North; Fourth Dynasty, probably reign of Khufu. Limestone with remains of paint, h. 28 cm (11 in.). The University of Pennsylvania Museum of Archaeology and Anthropology, Philadelphia (58-10-3)

33. *Hemiunu Seated.* Giza; Fourth Dynasty, later reign of Khufu. Limestone with remains of paint, h. 155.5 cm (61¼ in.). Roemer- und Pelizaeus-Museum, Hildesheim (1962)

34. *Reserve Head.* Giza; Fourth Dynasty, probably reign of Khufu. Limestone, h. 27.7 cm (10⅞ in.). Kunsthistorisches Museum, Ägyptische-Orientalische Sammlung, Vienna (ÄS 7787)

35. *Reserve Head.* Giza; Fourth Dynasty, probably reign of Khufu. Limestone, h. 30 cm (11⅞ in.). Museum of Fine Arts, Boston, Harvard University–Museum of Fine Arts Expedition (14.719)

36, 37. *Slab Stela of Prince Wep-em-nefret.* Giza; Fourth Dynasty, reign of Khufu. Limestone, h. 45.7 cm (18 in.). Phoebe Apperson Hearst Museum of Anthropology, University of California at Berkeley (6–19825)

38. *Princess Nefret-iabet.* Giza; Fourth Dynasty, reign of Khufu. Limestone, h. 37 cm (14⅝ in.). Staatliche Sammlung Ägyptischer Kunst, Munich (ÄS 7155)

39. *Slab Stela of Nefer.* Giza; Fourth Dynasty, reign of Khufu. Limestone with faint remains of paint, h. 38.1 cm (15 in.). Phoebe Apperson Hearst Museum of Anthropology, University of California at Berkeley (6–19801)

40. *Female Dancers and Musicians.* Giza; mid-Fourth to mid-Fifth Dynasty. Limestone, h. 78 cm (30¾ in.). Kunsthistorisches Museum, Ägyptisch-Orientalische Sammlung, Vienna (ÄS 8028)

41. *The Dwarf Per-ni-ankhu Seated.* Giza; Fourth Dynasty. Painted basalt, h. 48 cm (18⅞ in.). Egyptian Museum, Cairo (JE 98944)

42. *Head of King Djedefre.* Abu Rawash; Fourth Dynasty, reign of Djedefre. Red quartzite with remains of red paint, h. 26.5 cm (10⅜ in.). Musée du Louvre, Paris (E 12626)

43. *Small Head of a King, Probably Khafre, Wearing the White Crown.* Probably Giza; Fourth Dynasty, probably reign of Khafre. Dense beige limestone with inlaid eyes, h. 8 cm (3⅛ in.). Collection of Nanette B. Kelekian, New York

44. *King Khafre Seated.* Giza; Fourth Dynasty, reign of Khafre. Graywacke, h. 120 cm (47¼ in.). Egyptian Museum, Cairo (CG 15)

45. The Great Sphinx and King Khafre's pyramid, Giza

46. *Head of King Khafre*. Giza; Fourth Dynasty, reign of Khafre. Egyptian alabaster, h. 20.5 cm (8⅛ in.). Museum of Fine Arts, Boston, Harvard University–Museum of Fine Arts Expedition (21.351)

47. *Fragmentary Face of King Khafre*. Fourth Dynasty, reign of Khafre. Egyptian alabaster, h. 8.5 cm (3⅜ in.). The Metropolitan Museum of Art, New York, Purchase, Edward S. Harkness Gift, 1926 (26.7.1392)

48–52. *Group of Archers*. Reused at Lisht North; Fourth Dynasty, reigns of Khufu to Khafre. Painted limestone, h. 25.4 cm (10 in.). The Metropolitan Museum of Art, New York, Rogers Fund and Edward S. Harkness Gift, 1922 (22.1.23)

53. *Lady Khentet-ka and Her Son*. Giza; Fourth Dynasty, probably reign of Khafre. Limestone with remains of paint, h. 53 cm (20⅞ in.). Kunsthistorisches Museum, Ägyptisch-Orientalische Sammlung, Vienna (ÄS 7507)

54. *Head of an Older Man*. Mid-Fourth to early Fifth Dynasty. Painted limestone, h. 10.2 cm (4 in.). The Metropolitan Museum of Art, New York, Dodge Fund, 1947 (47.105.1)

55. *Triad of King Menkaure*. Giza; Fourth Dynasty, reign of Menkaure. Graywacke, h. 96 cm (37⅞ in.). Egyptian Museum, Cairo (JE 46499)

56. The pyramid of Menkaure at Giza, with remains of the pyramid temple

57, 58. *King Menkaure and a Queen*. Giza; Fourth Dynasty, reign of Menkaure. Graywacke, h. 139 cm (54¾ in.). Museum of Fine Arts, Boston, Harvard University–Museum of Fine Arts Expedition (11.1738)

59. *Stela of Ra-wer*. Giza; Fourth Dynasty, reign of Shepseskaf, or Fifth Dynasty, reign of Neferirkare. Egyptian alabaster with faint remains of paint, h. 85 cm (33½ in.). Egyptian Museum, Cairo (JE 6267)

60. See fig. 5.

61. *Pair Statue of Iai-ib and Khuaut*. Giza; Fourth Dynasty. Painted limestone, h. 73.5 cm (29 in.). Universität Leipzig, Ägyptisches Museum (3684)

62. *Pair Statue of Memi and Sabu*. Giza; Fourth Dynasty. Painted limestone, h. 62 cm (24⅜ in.). The Metropolitan Museum of Art, New York, Rogers Fund, 1948 (48.111)

63. *Pair Statue of Katep and Hetep-heres*. Probably Giza; Fourth Dynasty. Painted limestone, h. 47.5 cm (18¾ in.). Trustees of the British Museum, London (EA 1181)

64. *Four Statues of Inti-shedu*. Giza; end of Fourth Dynasty. Painted limestone, h. 31–75 cm (12¼–29½ in.). Egyptian Museum, Cairo (JE 98947, 98945, 98946, 98948)

65. *Head of King Userkaf*. Saqqara; Fifth Dynasty, reign of Userkaf. Red granite, h. 75 cm (29⅝ in.). Egyptian Museum, Cairo (JE 52501)

66, 67. *Running Troops*. Reused at Lisht North; Fifth Dynasty, reign of Userkaf. Limestone with faint remains of paint, h. 85 cm (33½ in.). The Metropolitan Museum of Art, New York, Rogers Fund, 1915 (15.3.1163)

68. *Two Birds*. Saqqara; Fifth Dynasty, reign of Userkaf. Painted limestone, h. 14.5 cm (5¾ in.). Egyptian Museum, Cairo (TEMP 6-9-32-1)

69. *Ship under Sail*. Reused at Lisht North; mid- to late Fourth or early Fifth Dynasty. Limestone with faint remains of paint, h. 72.8 cm (28⅝ in.). The Metropolitan Museum of Art, New York, Rogers Fund and Edward S. Harkness Gift, 1922 (22.1.13)

70, 71. *Sahure and a Nome God*. Fifth Dynasty, reign of Sahure. Gneiss, h. 64 cm (25¼ in.). The Metropolitan Museum of Art, New York, Rogers Fund, 1918 (18.2.4)

72, 73. *Models of the Pyramid Complex of King Sahure at Abusir*. Berlin, 1910. Made by Stegemann Brothers; restored by Ann Heywood, The Sherman Fairchild Center for Objects Conservation, and Ronald Street, Molding Studio, Metropolitan Museum, 1998. Wood, plaster, sand, and cardboard, (72) h. 62 cm (24½ in.); (73) h. 12 cm (5 in.); scale 1:75. The Metropolitan Museum of Art, New York, Dodge Fund, 1911 (11.165)

74, 75. *Relief Block with Deities and Fecundity Figures*. Abusir; Fifth Dynasty, reign of Sahure. Limestone with remains of paint, h., left side 137.5 cm (54⅛ in.), right side 132 cm (52 in.). Staatliche Museen zu Berlin, Ägyptisches Museum und Papyrussammlung (21784)

76, 77. *Running Troops*. Abusir; Fifth Dynasty, reign of Sahure. Limestone, total h. 86 cm (33⅞ in.). Sammlung des Ägyptologischen Instituts der Universität Heidelberg (HD 900)

78. *Lion-Headed Goddess Suckling King Niuserre*. Abusir, Fifth Dynasty, reign of Niuserre. Limestone with patches of ancient plaster and faint remains of paint, h. 112.2 cm (44¼ in.). Staatliche Museen zu Berlin, Ägyptisches Museum und Papyrussammlung (17911)

79. The sun temple of King Niuserre, Abu Ghurab. Computer reconstruction by David S. Johnson

80. *Early Summer in the Nile Valley, Relief Fragments*. Abu Ghurab; Fifth Dynasty, reign of Niuserre. Painted limestone, h. 72 cm (28⅜ in.). Staatliche Museen zu Berlin, Ägyptisches Museum und Papyrussammlung (20038)

81. *Jar Inscribed with the Name of King Unis*. Fifth Dynasty, reign of Unis. Egyptian alabaster, h. 17 cm (6¾ in.). Musée du Louvre, Paris (E 32 372)

82. *Starving Bedouin*. Saqqara; Fifth Dynasty, reign of Unis. Limestone with faint remains of paint, h. 38 cm (15 in.). Musée du Louvre, Paris (E 17 381)

83, 84. *Kai Seated*. Saqqara; probably early Fifth Dynasty. Painted limestone with inlaid eyes, h. 77 cm (30⅜ in.). Musée du Louvre, Paris (N 117 [= E 3024 = A 106])

85. *Snefru-nefer Standing*. Giza; late Fifth Dynasty. Painted limestone, h. 78 cm (30¾ in.). Kunsthistorisches Museum, Ägyptisch-Orientalische Sammlung, Vienna (ÄS 7506)

86. *Model of the Tomb of Per-neb*. Made 1916. The Metropolitan Museum of Art, New York. Original, Saqqara; Fifth Dynasty. The Metropolitan Museum of Art, New York, Gift of Edward S. Harkness, 1913 (13.183.3)

87. See fig. 2.

88, 89. *Pair Statue of Demedji and Henutsen*. First half of Fifth Dynasty. Painted limestone, h. 83 cm (32⅝ in.). The Metropolitan Museum of Art, New York, Rogers Fund, 1951 (51.37)

90, 91. *Ni-ka-re, His Wife, and Their Daughter*. Probably Saqqara; Fifth Dynasty, reign of Niuserre or later. Painted limestone, h. 57 cm (22½ in.). The Metropolitan Museum of Art, New York, Rogers Fund, 1952 (52.19)

92, 93. *Ni-ka-re, His Wife, and Their Son*. Saqqara; Fifth Dynasty, reign of Niuserre or later. Painted limestone, h. 57.5 cm (22⅝ in.). Brooklyn Museum of Art, Charles Edwin Wilbour Fund (49.215)

94. *Seked-kaw, His Wife, and Their Son*. Probably Saqqara; Fifth Dynasty, no later than reign of Niuserre. Painted limestone, h. 51 cm (20⅛ in.). Egyptian Museum, Cairo (CG 101)

95. *Butcher*. Said to be from Giza; Fifth Dynasty, probably reign of Niuserre. Limestone with remains of paint; knife restored, h. 37 cm (14⅝ in.). The Oriental Institute of The University of Chicago (10626)

96–99. *Potter*. Said to be from Giza; Fifth Dynasty, probably reign of Niuserre. Limestone with remains of paint, h. 13.2 cm (5¼ in.). The Oriental Institute of The University of Chicago (10628, 10645)

100, 101. *Nursing Woman*. Said to be from Giza; Fifth Dynasty, probably reign of Niuserre. Limestone with remains of paint, h. 10.5 cm (4⅛ in.). The Metropolitan Museum of Art, New York, Purchase, Edward S. Harkness Gift, 1926 (26.7.1405)

102. *Scribe*. Saqqara; Fifth Dynasty. Painted limestone, h. 49 cm (19⅜ in.). Egyptian Museum, Cairo (CG 78)

103, 104. *Carpenter and Market Scene from the Tomb of Tep-em-ankh*. Saqqara; first half of Fifth Dynasty, reign of Sahure or later. Limestone with remains of paint, (103) h. 30.5 cm (12 in.). Petrie Museum of Egyptian Archaeology, University College London (UC 14309); (104) w. 101 cm (39¾ in.). Egyptian Museum, Cairo (CG 1556)

105. *Relief of Itush*. Saqqara; Fifth Dynasty, reign of Djedkare Isesi. Limestone, h. 42.6 cm (16¾ in.). Brooklyn Museum of Art, Charles Edwin Wilbour Fund (37.25E)

106. *The Hunt in the Desert from the Tomb of Pehen-wi-ka*. Saqqara; mid-Fifth Dynasty, probably reign of Neferirkare or two following reigns. Limestone with remains of paint, h. 29 cm (11⅜ in.). Staatliche Museen zu Berlin, Ägyptisches Museum und Papyrussammlung (1132)

107. *The Hunt in the Desert from the Tomb of Ra-em-kai*. Saqqara; Fifth Dynasty, probably reign of Djedkare Isesi. Painted limestone, h. 92 cm (36¼ in.). The

Metropolitan Museum of Art, New York, Rogers Fund, 1908 (08.201.1g)

108. *Necklace*. Giza; Fifth Dynasty. Egyptian faience, l. 83 cm (32⅝ in.). Universität Leipzig, Ägyptisches Museum (3770)

109. *Bracelet*. Giza; late Fifth or early Sixth Dynasty. Egyptian faience, l. 16.5 cm (6½ in.). Kunsthistorisches Museum, Ägyptisch-Orientalische Sammlung, Vienna (ÄS 9073)

110. *Jar*. Mid-Fourth to mid-Fifth Dynasty. Egyptian alabaster, h. 33 cm (13 in.). The Metropolitan Museum of Art, New York, Rogers Fund, 1921 (21.2.8)

111. *Basin with Handle*. Giza; Sixth Dynasty. Copper, h. 10.5 cm (4⅛ in.). Universität Leipzig, Ägyptisches Museum (2169)

112, 113. *Sistrum Inscribed with the Name of King Teti*. Sixth Dynasty, reign of Teti. Egyptian alabaster with remains of pigment, h. 26.5 cm (10½ in.). The Metropolitan Museum of Art, New York, Purchase, Edward S. Harkness Gift, 1926 (26.7.1450)

114. *Queen Ankh-nes-meryre II and Her Son King Pepi II*. Sixth Dynasty, reign of Pepi II. Egyptian alabaster, h. 38.9 cm (15¼ in.). Brooklyn Museum of Art, Charles Edwin Wilbour Fund (39.119)

115. *King Pepi I Kneeling*. Sixth Dynasty, reign of Pepi I. Schist with inlaid eyes, h. 15.2 cm (6 in.). Brooklyn Museum of Art, Charles Edwin Wilbour Fund (39.121)

116. *Kneeling Captive*. Sixth Dynasty, reign of Pepi II. Limestone with remains of paint, h. 88.5 cm (34⅞ in.). The Metropolitan Museum of Art, New York, Fletcher Fund, 1947 (47.2)

117. *Fragment with Pyramid Texts*. Saqqara; Sixth Dynasty. Limestone with remains of paint, h. 24.5 cm (9⅝ in.). Petrie Museum of Egyptian Archaeology, University College London (UC 14540)

118. *Two Vases in the Shape of Mother Monkeys and Their Young*. Left: Sixth Dynasty, reign of Merenre. Egyptian alabaster, h. 18.5 cm (7¼ in.). The Metropolitan Museum of Art, New York, Theodore M. Davis Collection, Bequest of Theodore M. Davis, 1915 (30.8.134). Right: Sixth Dynasty, reign of Pepi I. Egyptian alabaster, h. 13.7 cm (5⅜ in.). The Metropolitan Museum of Art, New York, Purchase, Joseph Pulitzer Bequest, Fletcher Fund, and Lila Acheson Wallace, Russell and Judy Carson, William Kelly Simpson, and Vaughn Foundation Gifts, in honor of Henry George Fischer, 1992 (1992.338)

119. *Fishermen and Herdsmen with Their Animals*. Probably Saqqara; early Sixth Dynasty, reign of Teti or slightly later. Painted limestone. Left block, h. 47 cm (18½ in.); right block, h. 48.2 cm (19 in.). The Detroit Institute of Arts, City of Detroit Purchase (30.371)

120. *Still Life: Offerings for the Deceased*. Probably Saqqara; early Sixth Dynasty. Painted limestone, h. 48 cm (18⅞ in.). The Detroit Institute of Arts, Founders Society Purchase, Hill Memorial Fund (76.5)

121. *False-Door Stela from the Tomb of Metjetji*. Saqqara; Fifth Dynasty, reign of Unis, or early Sixth Dynasty. Limestone, h. 140 cm (55⅛ in.). The Metropolitan Museum of Art, New York, Gift of Mr. and Mrs. J. J. Klejman, 1964 (64.100)

122. *Fragment from the Facade of the Tomb of Metjetji*. Saqqara; Fifth Dynasty, reign of Unis, or early Sixth Dynasty. Painted limestone sculpted in sunk relief, h. 83 cm (32⅝ in.). Royal Ontario Museum, Toronto (953.116.1)

123. *Wall Painting from the Tomb of Metjetji*. Saqqara; Fifth Dynasty, reign of Unis, or early Sixth Dynasty. Paint on *muna* over a smoothed coating, h. 32 cm (12⅝ in.). Musée du Louvre, Paris (E 25 512)

124. *Meryre-ha-ishetef Standing*. Sedment; Sixth Dynasty. Painted ebony, h. 51 cm (20⅛ in.). Trustees of the British Museum, London (EA 55722)

125. *Atjema Standing*. Probably Saqqara; Sixth Dynasty. Painted limestone, h. 91 cm (35⅞ in.). Egyptian Museum, Cairo (CG 99)

126. *Meryre-ha-ishetef with a Staff*. Sedment; Sixth Dynasty. Painted cedar wood, h. 65.5 cm (25⅞ in.). Ny Carlsberg Glyptotek, Copenhagen (AEIN 1560)

127. *Prince Tjau Seated on the Ground*. Saqqara; Sixth Dynasty, reign of Merenre or later. Graywacke, h. 34.5 cm (13⅝ in.). Egyptian Museum, Cairo (CG 120)

BIBLIOGRAPHICAL NOTE

The main sources for the texts in this book were the essays and entries in *Egyptian Art in the Age of the Pyramids* (New York, 1999). Of the extensive bibliographical sources cited in that work the author is especially indebted to:

James P. Allen, "Re-wer's Accident," in *Studies in Pharaonic Religion and Society in Honour of J. Gwyn Griffiths*, edited by Alan B. Lloyd. London, 1992.

Jan Assmann, "Preservation and Presentation of Self in Ancient Egyptian Portraiture," in *Studies in Honor of William Kelly Simpson*, edited by Peter Der Manuelian, vol. 1. Boston, 1996.

Henry G. Fischer, "Anatomy in Egyptian Art," *Apollo* (July 1965), pp. 169–75.

Antonio Loprieno, "Der Sklave," in *Der Mensch im Alten Ägypten*, edited by Sergio Donadoni. Frankfurt,

1997. (The Italian-language original of this book was not available to the author.)

William Stevenson Smith, *A History of Egyptian Sculpture and Painting in the Old Kingdom*. 2nd ed. Boston and London. Reprinted, New York, 1978.

Nigel Strudwick, *The Administration of Egypt in the Old Kingdom: The Highest Titles and their Holders*. London and Boston, 1985.